TELL ME WHO I AM

Questions and Answers on Christian Spirituality

by

SUSAN ANNETTE MUTO and ADRIAN VAN KAAM

With FOREWORD and AFTERWORD

By

Adrian van Kaam

DIMENSION BOOKS
DENVILLE, NEW JERSEY 07834

First English Edition

Published by Dimension Books, Inc.

Denville, New Jersey, 07834

Imprimi Potest: Rev. Philip J. Haggerty, C.S.Sp.
                  Provincial

Nihil Obstat: Rev. William J. Winter, S.T.D.
                  Censor Librorum

Imprimatur: Most Rev. Vincent M. Leonard, D.D.
                  Bishop of Pittsburgh

                  January 11, 1977

L.C.C.C.No. 77-79224
ISBN 0-87193-000-5

CONTENTS

BOOKS BY ADRIAN VAN KAAM

A Light to the Gentiles
Religion and Personality
Personality Fulfillment in the Spiritual Life
Existential Foundations of Psychology
The Art of Existential Counseling
The Demon and the Dove (co-author)
Personality Fulfillment in the Religious Life
The Vowed Life
The Emergent Self (co-author)
The Participant Self (co-author)
On Being Involved
Envy and Originality
On Being Yourself
Spirituality and the Gentle Life
In Search of Spiritual Identity
Dynamics of Spiritual Self Direction
The Woman at the Well
Tell Me Who I Am (co-author)

BOOKS BY SUSAN ANNETTE MUTO

The Emergent Self (Co-author)
The Participant Self (Co-author)

Approaching the Sacred:
An Introduction to Spiritual Reading

Steps Along the Way:
The Path of Spiritual Reading

A Practical Guide to Spiritual Reading

Tell Me Who I Am (Co-author)

FOREWORD

By Adrian van Kaam

Christians today are in search of a spiritual self direction that may help them to cope meaningfully with the myriad problems they meet in themselves and in their surroundings. This search for self direction gives rise to many questions, such as those about life in community, acceptance of self, permanent commitment, prayer, personal feelings, religious life, and religious formation. This book attempts to give answers to several of the more central questions posed. To give answers in full would imply a more detailed explanation of the fundamentals of formative Christian spirituality. We try to deal fully with such matters in the academic program we offer at the Center for the Study of Spirituality of the Institute of Man at Duquesne University. There we are developing the religious science of formative spirituality. The practical side of that science implies a training of graduate students in the clear and attractive communication of the basics of Christian self direction they study in depth in their courses and seminars. Part of this training in speaking and writing entails work for our monthly journal ENVOY. The students try to incorporate with their own ideas the material of the Institute's courses. They draw upon this rich resource to answer the thousands of questions for direction that come to us at the Institute and through our field work in the USA and abroad. Their answers are worked over carefully by us as the editors of ENVOY and have proven to be of great help to a wide variety of readers.

Originally these questions were posed mainly by priests and religious. We discovered soon that their questions about Christian living in everyday life applied as well to many lay people. The latter read ENVOY and assured us that the questions and answers were so basic to the spiritual direction they were searching for that they applied not only to the life of clergy and religious but to any Christian eager to live a spiritual life in the modern world. Questions and answers about community life, that we thought would apply to religious more specifically, were to our pleasant surprise also read by the laity. For example, a young working woman with a leading position in a scientific laboratory visited us recently. She came to tell us that she got most out of the questions and answers regarding life in community. She told us that in the community of the laboratory and in the community of her friends who form the small crew of the sailboat she owns the same tensions arose as mentioned in the questions of religious. She felt better able to cope effectively as a Christian with these tensions in light of her reflections upon the answers she found in ENVOY.

It is for this reason that we hope readers in all walks of life will apply to their own self direction the questions and answers that turn around the problems faced by religious. We invite every reader to reflect personally on the content of this book and to dialogue with it in light of his or her particular situation in family and world.

The initial material for this book emerged from the supervised and extensively edited work of the students and graduates whom we gratefully acknowledge below. For this publication, however, Dr. Muto and I have carefully worked over and integrated their answers to bring them more perfectly in tune with our original lectures, spiritual self theory, previous publications, and awareness of the needs of a new readership. As a matter of fact, *Tell Me Who I Am* is a whole new book that may lead you to a renewed discovery of who you are and of how you can live for Christ in every walk of life. In light of this quest, you may want to search further and be led to other publications by the authors that deepen and expand the material presented here. This book may serve as a first practical initiation in the art and discipline of spiritual self direction and the questioning and reflecting it entails. To facilitate this initiation, I conclude this book with an afterword on finding your unique life destiny in the Lord.

In closing we gratefully acknowledge the ENVOY work done by the following former students, research associates, and graduates of the Center for the Study of Spirituality, of which we serve respectively as director and assistant director: Fr. Paul Bovankovich; Sr. Barbara Breaud, O. Carm.; Fr. Richard Byrne, OCSO; Sr. Bernadette Casey, RSM; Fr. Daniel Crosby, OFM Cap; Sr. Bernardine Dirkx, SSM; Sr. Mary Agnes Earner, SDR; Sr. Ann Christine Elia, OSF; Sr. Mary Bethany Fitzgerald, SSJ; Sr. M. Rose Clarisse Gadoury, SSA; Fr. Barnabas Gorski, OFM; Dr. Carolyn Gratton; Sr Louise Hageman, OP, Sr. Marie Colette Hanlon, SC; Br. Martin Helldorfer, FSC; Sr. Maureen Kelly, SSL; Sr. Geraldine Klein, SHG; Sr. Marilyn Kuzmickus, SSC; Fr. Richard LaMadeleine, MS; Sr. Barbara Nell Laperouse, O. Carm.; Sr. Shawn Lee, SSJ; Sr. Clare McKeever, SSL; Sr. Julia Norton, CSJ; Fr. Anthony O'Connell, OSM; Sr. Katherine O'Toole, SC; Sr. Margaret Perring, SSJ; Sr. Johan Michele Rake, CDP; Sr. Sharon Richardt, DC; Sr. Mary Satala, DC; Sr. Romayne Schaut, OSB; Sr. Mary Blaise Semple, SJSM; Sr. Miriam Sharpe, RSM; Fr. William Sheehan, OMI; Sr. Sarah Marie Sherman, RSM; Sr. Elaine Smurawa, SSJ; Sr. Fidelis Tracy, CDP; Sr. Esther Warren, OP; Sr. Jane Zawadski, SSJ; Fr. Clement Zeleznik, OSB; Sr. Christine Zimorski, SSJ.

ABOUT THE AUTHORS

ADRIAN VAN KAAM is a renowned spiritual writer and professor of spirituality as an academic and practical discipline. After a period of teaching and studying the psychology of spirituality, during which he received a doctoral degree at Case Western Reserve University, he was able in 1963 to dedicate himself to his main interest—research, teaching, and publication in the field of formative spirituality. Father van Kaam is presently professor of spirituality in the Center for the Study of Spirituality, of which he is founder and director. He is editor of the journals HUMANITAS and ENVOY, author of over 100 articles and 17 books, including *Religion and Personality; Spirituality and the Gentle Life;* and *Dynamics of Spiritual Self Direction.*

*

*

SUSAN ANNETTE MUTO, who holds a doctorate in English literature, is assistant director of the Institute and coordinator of its master's program in formative fundamental spirituality. She is also managing editor of the Center's monthly spiritual journal, ENVOY, and of HUMANITAS, the tri-yearly journal of the Institute's Center for the Study of Human Development. She is the author of several articles and books, including *Approaching the Sacred; Steps Along the Way*; and *A Practical Guide to Spiritual Reading.*

QUESTIONS AND ANSWERS
on
I. LIFE IN COMMUNITY

Action and Acceptance

Speaking One's Mind

Present-Day Emotional Problems

Living with a Group of Compatible People

Achieving Creative Communication in Community

* * *

Action and Acceptance

Is the true religious attitude solely one of passive acceptance of our situation and sufferings in community life or is there a place for active attempts to better our world and more particularly our religious community?

* * *

The younger members of a community seem inclined to activity. The older are more prone to be passive. While the older are satisfied with the world they built, the younger are more sensitive to its shortcomings. To the older everything might look all right. To the younger everything might look all wrong.

Totalizing on either side is equally false. The present situation includes both past and future. My community is time-bound. In this situation, I am faced with the choice of either accepting things as they are or striving to improve them.

The dilemma to act or not to act is not easily solved. At the peak of enthusiasm, I usually lack the distance necessary to make a wise and lasting decision. My needs may influence my choice to act quickly rather than to evaluate all sides.

I may especially go wrong if I attempt to change *quickly* and *completely* the structure of my community as it presently exists. I may question this structure but generally I should work within it to bring about a gradual change. Working within the structure safeguards me against my own needs for popularity, power, prestige, or whatever onesided perspective clouds my vision of the whole.

I should thus listen to events as they are taking place presently in light of the past and future. I should not be oblivious to the deficiencies of my community. Neither should I be blinded by the demands of my own needs. Rather my aim should be to focus on what I can do creatively and realistically at this time to truly renew my community. Destroying it will not help.

It may be that I should accept existing circumstances for the time being. On the other hand, I may be called to do something now. The practical decision about when and how to act can be extremely difficult. This is particularly true when the changes I am proposing seem to counter what others consider to be the purpose and meaning of religious life. Then I ought to stop and reconsider a basic question:

Is it possible that I have identified a project of my own with the purpose of religious life and as a result blocked out all that does not coincide with my private plan? Is what I think best for the betterment of the community actually only for my own betterment?

If I can sincerely say "no" to this question and feel convinced that I am concerned with more basic issues, it is helpful to ponder another possibility. An initial jolt may be necessary and someone has to take the risk, but am I the person to do so at this time and under these circumstances?

Ultimately I have to decide when and in what way to act, and this decision will reflect the orientation of my life as a whole. If I permeate my life with prayerful presence to the Divine. I can be poised for action when there is a call without being pressured by the demand for success. Perhaps mine can be described as a life of serene dynamism, with a serenity stemming from prayerful reflection that is, at the same time, in tune with the dynamic movements of life around me.

At times passive acceptance is best; other times may call for more forceful activity. All I can know for sure is that I must try to be open to what is best for each person and for the community as a whole at this time. I can then see the wisdom of distancing myself from my plans long enough to appraise them in a personal way. I neither accept things passively nor dominate them compulsively. Rather I attempt to take into consideration all aspects of life in the community to which I belong.

Respectful listening is impossible without some surrender to the structures of my situation. Surrender does not mean cynical endurance nor an unrealistic pretense that problems do not exist. Neither does action always imply gaining the upper hand. Rather my religious self responds most fully when I seek to discover in the situation the deeper roots of my community in the Divine.

Presence to the Holy reveals to me that I am in the world not only to create it anew in tune with time and place but also to endure patiently what I am unable to improve. Paradoxically, production becomes more meaningful in light of relaxation; dynamism finds its deepest ground in recollection. Christ becomes the inspiration of both participation and recollection, the orientation of activity and resignation, the background of production and relaxation.

Living this rhythm of action and contemplation is likely not only to inspire others but also to make my efforts to improve the community more sincere and acceptable to members of all ages. In His light, we may move toward living in unity despite our differences, knowing all the while that the perfectly harmonious community is on earth no where to be found.

* * *

Speaking One's Mind

In our community there seems to be a negative sanction against speaking one's mind. How can we be open to one another and honest enough to have the courage of our convictions? Is sensitivity training the answer?

* * *

Currently we are caught in enthusiasm for encounter and community. We are eager to arrange group experiences, conduct sensitivity sessions, change structures that hinder communication, establish forms of living conducive to dialogue and openness. Yet, with the passage of time, having experimented extensively, many religious still find themselves empty, unintegrated, and often quite lonely.

Three "types" seem to emerge: the fearful, the frantic, the free.

As a fearful religious, I feel compelled to rigidly structure my life. Perfection for me means the exact performance of duty, the compulsive observance of devotional practices. I have learned to cover up my emotions and control my life. In the past I found security in the structures of religious life. Now these structures are changing. Even the experts are advocating a loosening of the rule. I am afraid to say anything. I feel anxious and defensive. I distrust the young who seem to be telling me that my life lacks meaning; I distrust the old who refuse to listen to my disparaging remarks. I feel frightfully alone.

Caught in the turmoil of contemporary religious life, I may become not fearful and afraid to let go of the past but frantic and incapable of remaining peacefully in the present. I live outside of myself, always looking for the latest remedy to reduce the ills of the world. To prove how relevant I am, I try desperately to keep up with current trends in teaching, theology, technique. I am so busy being busy that I fail to be present to anything in depth. I feel exceedingly empty and the more I try to fill the void with any temporary solution that presents itself the emptier I feel. At the root of my restlessness may lie the hidden conviction that I am capable of redeeming myself.

As a religious who is truly free, I live both within myself, in humble presence to the Lord, and outside myself as an embodiment of His love in the world. The person of Christ is never far from my own person. I can communicate with others because I am in touch with my deepest core. I try to see all sides of the situation. Aware of my own limitations, I feel compassion for every religious in my community—the reticent as well as the talkative, the fearful as well as the frantic. I recognize that a genuine meeting between persons is always rooted in recollected self-presence before the Lord.

Christian love between persons is reborn in solitude: we who are alone can reach those from whom we have been separated by misunderstanding, anger, irritation because we find the core of our unity in Christ. Presence to the Divine Word makes it possible for us to break through the walls that isolate man from man. One hour of solitude may bring us closer to those with whom we live than many hours of forced communication.

Techniques alone do not remedy man's inability to communicate with his fellow man. They may have some beneficial results, but the blind appropriation of any technique is always dangerous. Perhaps before saying that sensitivity training is the answer, I ought to ask myself why I am running after so many techniques in an effort to become open. Am I afraid to face myself and accept my own failings? Is lack of openness in others toward me a result of my lack of openness toward them? Such honest searching does not simply mean speaking what is on my mind; it implies a readiness to speak as well as a waiting to be spoken to. It is believing that I know something while admitting that I do not know everything.

Honesty and openness toward others thus begins by being honest and open with myself. Too often, however, in my haste to achieve community, my forceful approach only pushes people farther apart. Group methods and pressures may foster cozy togetherness but may destroy the possibility of true community, the purpose of which is to protect each member and give him the opportunity for personal and spiritual growth.

Only when I have experienced the communion of solitude can I come to know the joy of union with others. I will then have the courage to live my convictions and, when appropriate, to present them to the group without fear of ridicule.

The community which is created on basis of respectful presence to each person cannot be attained by group processes alone. As well-intentioned and carefully structured as sensitivity sessions may be, they remain only a technique for community living, which may have good or bad effects depending on the variables. However, life in community cannot be based on technique alone. Unless it is rooted in an intense and continuing self-knowledge—gleaned from others and from the silence of meeting Christ in solitude—there can be no lasting honesty and integrity.

* * *

Present-Day Emotional Problems

We seem to be having more emotional problems in our present-day communities than we had in the past. As an older religious, I feel that the controlled environment of a few years ago was healthier emotionally than the personal decision and uncertainty our present uncontrolled environment engenders. Could you comment please?

* * *

" . . . let it be past . . . and it is at once idealized." Thoreau's words are as true today as when he wrote them. Everyone tends to turn nostalgically to the good old days.

How simple things were then. Television had not invaded our lives. Teenagers never dreamed of rebelling against established institutions. Blacks were "colored folk" who knew how to keep their place . . .

The simple fact is that those days are gone forever. I cannot idealize the past and expect to prepare myself for the present, to say nothing of meeting the challenge of the future. If I look only to what was, I cannot plan for what will be nor can I enjoy the unique experience of living what is. Religious are part of the present culture and not simply carry-overs from an idyllic past.

Are the rapid changes in religious life as unhealthy as I fear? Many religious are experiencing emotional problems. Some may even require professional help. What I feel is not unlike the fear parents must feel when they send their first son off to college. Will he be able to cope with his new-found freedom? What if he forgets the rules of good conduct taught to him at home? No one can calm the fears of parents by telling them that nothing will go wrong once their son is on campus. There is just no guarantee.

Parents might decide to keep their son at home but sheltering him is no solution. He may end up feeling hostile toward his parents for protecting him from the pain of personal decision. Emotional problems may arise which never would have arisen had he gone to college and faced the rude awakening of campus life.

Refusing to create the conditions of risk and responsibility in which people can grow would likewise compound the problems in religious life. Emotional disturbances might be "overlooked in charity." Under the guise of being a good religious, I might keep my anger and hostility to myself. So carefully hidden are my emotions that the leaders of my community may fail to recognize severe disturbances and simply advise me to pray more. However, genuine prayerfulness, as opposed to lock-step piety, may be impossible if I do not consider my feelings.

I may obey the rule in a rigid and mechanical fashion, becoming in the process more and more alienated from my emotional life. Inevitably, I feel confused and unhappy when structures change. Perhaps for the first time since I entered community, I am thrown back upon myself. I have to decide when to pray, how much money to spend, what kind of dress to wear. My inability to make these decisions may be traceable to my family background, where all major choices were made for me. Later, when I entered religious life, I may have been the product of a faulty formation program which, because of its detailed rigidity, deprived me of the necessary opportunity to make decisions and protected me from the healthy experience of living in doubt, denial, and uncertainty.

It is not enough to listen to myself; I must also listen to the culture in which I live. In years past, people lived in a more agrarian, less automated culture. Their lives in small towns and villages were in practice more personal. God was their familiar as much as their fellow man. Hence they had little objection to formalized prayer. Their lives revolved around the mysterious forces of wind, soil, and rain; so they sought security in the regular routines of religious practice.

Today man has mastered many of nature's forces but the gnawing experience of a Presence beyond his control still persists. Because he lives in a complex, controlled society, which separates man from man, he desires to meet the other and God in a more personal way. The scene has changed but the motivation for worship remains the same: the raising of one's mind and heart to God.

All of this seems to say that a retreat from the present to the past is no answer for today's religious. Perhaps what is called for is a more realistic formation program, one in which young and old alike could develop respect for the wisdom of the past, an openness to the promise of the future, and an ability to live in peace with the fear and uncertainty of the present.

Today I am faced with the challenge of responding in a personal way to the unique call of Christ. I realize that my personal call from Him did not end on the day I entered community. Christ's call comes to me moment by moment. I must be alert to the inspiration of the Spirit speaking to me in prayer, in my profession, and in the people with whom I associate. Fidelity to my vocation involves risk and conflict but where there is tension there is life.

Confusion can give rise to good questions for reflection. Why do I get upset when others are not doing what I think they should? Are my doubts about religious life real or rooted in fantasy? Have I faced fully the consequences of giving up my commitment? Am I willing to talk to someone I trust about my problems? Will I be able to listen to what he has to say? Can I stand alone if necessary? Am I honestly searching for God's will in my life or are my desires clouded by anxious self-preoccupation and a restless dissatisfaction with the imperfections of my community?

Such prayerful reflection alone or with others requires painful effort and honesty, but dwelling on my feeling life, under the proper direction, may prove to be a fine way of deepening my spiritual life. And, to quote Saint Irenaeus, "The glory of God is man fully alive."

* * *

Living with a Group of Compatible People

I think that living in a group where one is with compatible people would be conducive to religious life. My superior thinks I am naive about friendships and is unwilling to form an experimental community on the basis of compatibility.

Am I wrong to foster such a life style? If so, what can I do to make our environment at home more religious?

* * *

No doubt the thought has occurred to me that if I could only choose my living companions most of my problems in community would dissolve. If only I could live with my friends, tensions would disappear and I would be happier, holier and apostolically more effective.

In theory this solution sounds ideal. But is it realistic? And is it really the best thing for me to live only with those for whom I feel a certain affinity?

In my desire to experiment, I may fail to take into account the financial situation of my community. I want only to forge ahead, forgetting its customs and traditions, overlooking the life history of its members.

If I choose to associate only with compatible people, I may be following a course which for all its smoothness prevents personal growth. Friends who never rock my boat are poor navigators. They never ask me to question my motives or ideals, but allow me to drift aimlessly with the tides of the time and my own temporary whims.

A real friend would not only encourage me to follow my goals. He would caution me when he thinks I am wrong. I do not notice my blind spots but he does. Furthermore, if friendship is genuine, living with my friend is not absolutely necessary. Communications between us may be frequent or sparse, but our friendship is deep enough to withstand any distance. We are present to one another even in absence.

In some cases, communities founded on compatible friendships have been beneficial; in other cases the "friendship" community had to be abandoned. A whole complex of reasons caused the breakup. The failure of the experiment does not necessarily mean the persons involved were naive about friendship; it could mean they were naive about religious life.

Religious life involves an attempt to uncover and dwell on the meaning of God in my life and in my relations with others. Friendship is a gift. To make it a project is just as manipulative as to plan the kind of community to which I will commit myself. Friendship is not the basic reason for coming together in community; neither is it the main motivating force of staying together.

On what is community living really based? I may join educational, civic and social groups for a variety of reasons, but none of these would be sufficient to hold together that group of persons which constitute a religious community. Each religious responds not to one or the other contemporary need but to a divine call to commit himself to the Eternal Word. The essence of the bond that unites us is, as Chardin says, "the single attraction to the same Someone."

A religious community never exists as an end in itself. It is a means to help each religious live more fully for Christ and to witness for His way in the world.

Tensions are facts of life in community living. They are unavoidable whenever persons—no matter how friendly or saintly—live in close proximity. Yet they play a positive role in human development. Tensions will arise to the degree that I retain my inner core of uniqueness. I should not expect a total reduction of tension even in interactions with my best friend.

No one would deny that being with a friend brings with it a feeling of relaxation and release. We enjoy each other's company, think alike on most issues but feel free to vocalize our differences. We seek mutual support and understanding. As time passes we come to know one another more intimately. New sides of our personality come to the fore. Our masks fall off. We see each other as we really are.

In revealing myself, there is an ever-present risk. If my friend knows me as I really am, will he still love me? I can never answer this question in advance: I can only believe and trust.

Living with others thus involves tension; friends are no exception. In fact, because we mean so much to one another, our differences can be magnified. The deeper I am bound to someone in love, the more I suffer from my own jealousy, anger and hostility toward him. Not even the most intimate relationship between husband and wife preserves them from experiencing tension.

Restricting my community experience to living comfortably with my friends may seem attractive but it could lessen my possibility for personal growth. Personhood develops in relationship, and, as Hopkins reminds us,

> . . . Christ plays in ten thousand places,
> Lovely in limbs, and lovely in eyes not his
> To the Father through the features of men's faces.

Unlike the Jewish people of the Old Testament, I miss seeing the hand of God in every situation. I am inclined to draw lines between the psychological me and the religious me, between what daily life is all about and what eternity has to do with it.

In the spiritual life such splitting is overcome. The psychological me and the religious me are intertwined. Time is not one day isolated from the next but time proceeding into eternity. All that I am and all that my community is are bound together in the whole and Holy. I can live with others in spiritual communion without necessarily experiencing personal compatibility. But . . .
. . . Sister Jane finds fault with whatever people say. Sister Patricia seems to have lost all desire to pray. Sister Karen never cracks a smile. Am I supposed to accept this situation

as it is? The answer is yes.

My celibate commitment did not guarantee that I would always live with compatible people. It was a promise that I would try to see what lies beneath the troubled waters of human togetherness. To be celibate in Christ is to be in harmony with myself and others in the deepest ground of our being. To be celibate in Christ is to live with others in respectful love, to look again at Sister Jane, Sister Patricia, and Sister Karen. Jane may not know how to relate to people in a positive way. Deep down Patricia would like to pray but for now she has to live through her own dark night. And so on with Karen and all the rest.

Instead of focusing on personal compatibility—which cannot be forced—perhaps I should think about what makes an environment religious. A simple answer would be that what matters is not making the environment more religious but being more of a religious in the present environment. Surely care ought to be shown for one another's needs for privacy and quiet times as well as for supportive togetherness at meals and during times of prayer and recreation. But the question I need to reexamine most is whether or not the spiritual dimension still holds primacy in my life?

As a religious I am at home when I allow God to be the center of my life. In this center I come to rest. From it I move out into the world. When my home in God is solid and strong, I can feel secure in any situation.

I do not expect an earthly community to be tailored to suit exactly the needs and preferences of each member. On the contrary, religious community is that place where many different persons, who share the same center in Christ, come together to live and work and embody in the world their experience of dwelling with the Divine. Neither the physical plant nor the particular persons who inhabit this place are looked upon as prerequisites for community.

A true religious community is only possible when presence to Christ is central in each of our lives. Such a community is marked by a peace and calm which rises from within. It does not come about by frantically making a project of forming friendships. More than establishing artificial standards of compatibility, life centers around prayer which becomes the integrating and inspiriting core of all that we do and decide.

Such an atmosphere cannot be forced but neither does it come about by chance. Each religious is responsible for its creation. To the extent that we root our lives in God and truly care for one another, we will be able to feel at home in our religious communities.

To live in acceptance of the human condition and all its potential is to live religiously. For being human means living every moment with tragedies and graces at my fingertips. It means trying to feel at home in all kinds of unsettling situations. Accepting the freedom and surprises of every human endeavor. Knowing that anything can happen to me. Being human means being a bearer of the cross. Hoping, believing, and living with a Savior who is difficult to recognize in our world today. Reaching out to the person next to me and risking the pain of an empty grasp. Being human is a feeling of fulfillment in joy, love, and grace; it is also the experience of emptiness, dissatisfaction, and dismay.

Wherever the experience of full human living exists, Christ is to be found. The atmosphere of such a home is permeated by a faith that believes in the growing depth of life which culminates in Christ. This shared faith, which must be concretized in daily prayer, worship, work and play, is the invisible peace and joy of all those who share the intimacy of a religious home.

When I am able to respect others and myself for who and what we are and for who and what we can become, I will find that I have no need to pick and choose those with whom I want to live. Within the totality of the whole and Holy, each person has his own dignity, his own destiny.

Dag Hammarskjöld once remarked, "Unless we each find a way to chime in as one note in the organic whole, we shall only observe ourselves observing the interplay of its thousand components . . . " It is for each of us to help the other actualize that dignity, to accomplish that destiny.

* * *

Achieving Creative Communication in Community

I entered religious life because I felt I could do in community what I could not do as an individual. Yet year after year I find that I am living with people with whom I cannot communicate. I often do not feel any kinship with those in my house. I have so little in common with them. What hope is there for creative communication and the achievement of common goals?

* * *

A clipping from a recent newspaper column reads: "What has happened to our marriage? We do not communicate at all any more. We hardly have time to talk and be together since he has taken a second job. Now he must go to California for the summer, and I'll be left alone with the children. What's wrong? Why haven't we found in marriage the happiness we expected?"

Happiness, whether in marriage or religious life, may always elude me if my expectations of others are unrealistic. Perhaps I want my world to be a perfect one in which I am treated kindly by everyone and communicate with little effort. In this dream world, everything would be planned by me and operate according to my designs. Since no such utopia is to be found, I live suspended between the real and the ideally expected.

Underlying the question of communication and community is thus a more basic issue: What are my expectations of religious life? Can I, as a member of this community, find meaning in a situation which seems empty, personally draining and void of possibilities for personal fulfillment? Asking this question means that I have to question the reasons why I entered religious life in the first place. Did I respond to an appeal clothed in mystery which directed me to dedicate my life to Christ and to the service of His Church?

The call was clear but the way was shrouded in mystery. The only direction I had was the Lord's own words: "Sell all you have and give to the poor. You will have treasure in heaven. Then come and follow me" (Luke 18:22). He promised me no success, no comforts. He asked only one question: Would I listen to His will for me as He chose to manifest Himself in the people, things, and events I would meet along the way? Did I say yes to Christ, or was I seeking a place where I could actualize myself in a merely humanistic sense?

If I find myself feeling that others ought to be more understanding of me, that there ought to be a more friendly atmosphere in our house, that fellow religious ought to affirm my creativity, then perhaps I am only engaging in a narcissistic search for self-fulfillment. I long for the secure and simple world of childhood. Then communication was easy. Support came through an approving smile that said I was behaving well, admonition through a disapproving frown that told me I was being bad. I could then adjust my behavior accordingly.

Adult life is more complex. However, without mitigating the problems of communication, I may discover that in most cases they stem at least in part from unrealistic expectations, from childish needs for affirmation which demand of others a consistent response they cannot give. I am bound to experience disappointment when love and praise is lacking. Nonetheless, disillusionment can be a path toward more personal living, depending on my attitude.

Disagreements are part of the cross Christ asked me to bear for His sake. Harboring high expectations may destroy the possibility of seeing the good that is present in each unique self. In such a frame of mind, I cannot help but feel discouraged when we fail to communicate.

Instead of measuring communication by the yardstick of consensus, I ought to ask myself if I am willing to receive others as they are, knowing full well that I am not the only one carrying my cross for Him, that the crosses of others may be far heavier than the one I have been asked to bear.

Surely I ought to make reasonable efforts to remedy an unhappy home situation but waiting for the other to make the first move may be foolhardy. I cannot willfully change others but I can change myself. If I live the apparently humdrum moments in an inspirited way, the same old thing can become a source of new life. Even a discussion about the laundry can be an avenue of creative communication when I put my heart in it. But most of the time my concerns are elsewhere. I expend so much energy seeking an ideal encounter that I miss the wonder of everyday.

Trying too hard to communicate can be another reason for the problem of non-communication. There is much talk and little silence, many occasions for encounter and few to be alone, space for sharing but lack of space for privacy. Communication seems to be equated with quantity rather than quality. The hidden assumption of this trend is that the more language I use the more successful I will be in transmitting my message.

Experience refutes this assumption. On many occasions, I find myself frustrated and saying, "I can't get through to him!" "I don't know how else to say it so that he will understand!" Theoretically, however, I may continue to act as if using words efficiently is enough to insure creative communication.

How can I cut through mere verbiage and reach the other? Emily Dickinson hints at one way in her brief poem:

A word is dead
When it is said, some say:
I say it just begins to live—
That day.

Words, she says, take on life and meaning only when men speak them. Too often I forget that the words I speak come alive only after I inspirit them. The source of their life is my own living.

Two contrasting approaches to words might be those of Mary and Mark. Mary goes after others with the intention of communicating with them. She is skillful in verbal techniques and is always trying them out. Mark's attitude with others is open and respectful. Mary views them in terms of her own needs. For all her skill, she may not be able to receive the gift of self the other is holding out. Her specialized vocabulary is not wide enough to embrace the other as he really is.

Mark is more likely than Mary to find a person with whom he can communicate precisely because he is not willfully looking for such a person. He has not reduced the value of the other to his capacity to communicate. Rather he lets the other be in his uniqueness. In such an atmosphere of appreciation, the person is more easily drawn to share what is of value to him. The chances for creative communication to occur are thus greatly increased.

However I may hunger for someone with whom to share the things I find most meaningful in life, finding such a person cannot be made a willful project. Creative communication is a gift I can neither earn nor demand. I can only ready myself to receive this gift when it comes. Demian says in Hesse's novel of the same title that "genuine communion is a beautiful thing. The real spirit will come from the knowledge that separate individuals have of one another and for a time it will transform the world."

I go to the other for his own sake, not for what he can do to further my ambitions and desires or because he can alleviate my fears. Rather I am with him because his existence really matters to me. I am therefore other-oriented, humbly grateful for those moments when, despite all reasons to the contrary, we are able to touch one another and be touched in a significant way.

This personal approach is not easy since it requires a deep trust of the other as other. I must accept him as he is, with his weaknesses as well as his strengths. Although I may delight in the ways in which we are alike, I also discover that we are different. In many ways the other is not me. Thus I experience a oneness with him and, at the same time, a complementary experience of the uniqueness of myself. This discovery prompts me not to impose my ideas on him but to trust the personal unfolding of who he is.

The words I speak cannot be utterances chosen from an accumulated vocabulary. They must be words of life that issue from the heart. Creative communication does not come from outside me but from within. It is the merging of my life with my words and with the Word—not a proliferation of verbal techniques but the mutual engagement of persons in the Body of Christ, at once respectful of each member and of all the members together.

QUESTIONS AND ANSWERS

on

II. ACCEPTANCE OF SELF

Learning to Accept Myself

Living Up to an Idealized Self-Image

Relying on External Forms of Devotionalism and Behaviorism

* * *

Learning to Accept Myself

If I do not accept myself, is it because of pride—wanting to be perfect? Do I lack a sense of self-worth? How can I learn to accept myself?

* * *

The main reason why I cannot accept myself may be because I want to be somebody I am not. My ideal self would be patient, understanding, open to different opinions. I would never be angry, impatient or irritated. Always loving, never spiteful, that's how I want to be.

In accordance with my ideal self-image, I may never express a contradictory opinion. Such expression would entail loss of the other's good will. I may never oppose the other. Opposition would destroy the rapport I have established between us. My pride does not permit anger under any circumstances.

Clearly I do not accept my real self when I live under the tyranny of an ideal self-image.

Failure to know myself may also arise from the tendency to view myself in ultimate terms. I dislike the uncertainty of being *somewhat* intelligent, *somewhat* efficient, *somewhat* generous. I long to be perfectly brilliant, masterfully organized, radiantly generous. Experience tells me, however, that my position is far more ambiguous.

There is confusion and clutter in my personality. My noblest deeds may be motivated by willful pride, my humblest acts shadowed by envy and jealousy. Only slowly do I begin to discover the height and depth of the mystery which I am.

Acceptance of self presupposes this discovery of who I am

and what I am called to be. Discovery of self is a lifelong endeavor made doubly difficult by my propensity for self-deception. Many and devious are the paths of deception which lead me away from my true self.

Recall, for instance, the feeling of elation which comes over me when someone I like praises me. This feeling is fine in itself. However, I alone know the little tricks I have devised to warrant this praise, even when it is undeserved. In order to command this person's attention, I slightly exaggerated the details of my daring enterprise. I certainly did not set out intentionally to deceive him. I only wanted to insure his undivided attention.

It is human to feel happy when I receive deserved praise, but I should not deceive myself about the seductive ploys I used to bind the other's attention. I wanted to have the last word and so I subtly directed the conversation around to the part I played in his plan, stressing in the meantime the hardships under which I had to work. The praise I felt I deserved was granted to me, but the price I had to pay for it was high.

Pride posing as humility is one of the most elusive forms of self-deception.

If I concentrate only on what I regard as praiseworthy in my personality, I may be subject to pride. If, on the contrary, I attend only to my weaknesses, I may become discouraged. To be realistic, I have to see all sides of myself, cease demanding perfection, and open up to my need for relaxed acceptance of what makes me, "me."

When I take a good look at myself, no longer seeing only my negative, undesirable qualities, no longer looking at myself in comparison to others more capable than I, I begin to discover that in spite of my inadequacies, I am of real worth and value as a person. Even those things about me I hated to admit, I can now view as areas for potential growth.

I can look back on an incident that aroused my anger. I was angry then and have been angry before under similar circumstances. Why deny it? Why not accept myself as a person capable of feeling anger? It is not necessary to act out my anger to achieve this acceptance. Recognition of the feeling as my own is enough to initiate an accepting stance.

Integrating this feeling into my life comes later; accepting the feeling as mine comes first.

This acceptance happens gradually; I cannot force it to take place. As I try to be open to all the feelings I experience, I soon begin to value the unique self I am. Being more my own person, I am freer from false pride, more capable of being present to myself and others.

Self-acceptance can never be a solitary act. A dialogue goes on at all times between what I am and what I am becoming.

The self I am at present depends on my past. Parents, family, school, neighborhood, religious affiliation—all play a part in what I know of myself and of my relation to the world. I come to know myself through my relation with others, yet I am always distinct from them.

I discover myself always in this twofold movement: I go out of myself to meet events, people, and things; I return to myself in solitude to distinguish myself from those around me and from the pressures they exert upon me to be other than what I am.

If my search for myself is sincere, I must be willing to accept what I discover: the needs, desires and passions that may narrow my possibility for growth as well as those that may facilitate self-emergence.

As I grow in self-understanding, it becomes easier for me to accept myself—not as I would like to be, or as others would have me be, but as I am.

The joyful, liberating moment when I accept me as "me" does not come by tabulating my positive and negative qualities. Self-acceptance involves my whole person, not just my calculating intellect. I can never accept myself unless I know that I am accepted by others and by God: others whose honest concern and interest I cannot doubt; God who created me and by this act manifested his eternal acceptance of me.

A longtime friend or counselor, colleague or spiritual director who knows my strong and weak points and still accepts me, helps me to experience myself as acceptable. Such a person does not gloss over or agree with my undesirable characteristics. He accepts me in my totality. He does not pick and choose.

When I forget myself for others, when I recognize their needs and accept them in their totality, I realize the power I have for doing some good. I see it in the face and grateful smile of another.

Gradually I realize that I who am the source of good and love for others must somehow be good and loveable myself. And again it happens: through others, as through God, I receive the gift of self-acceptance.

As a Christian, this gift of acceptance stands out in its full splendor. Through Christ's passion and death, I am gifted with a love that redeems me from my divisive self, with a grace that renews me and invites me to be the self I am called to be from time and eternity.

Long after I have ceased being useful to others, I can still accept myself, for this poor limited me, who has failed so many times, is infinitely loved by the Lord. He became man to redeem me and to help me find and embody the will of the Father for me.

Thus I am called to accept myself as He accepted me. When I fail Him, I fail myself. When I find myself, I also find Him whose loving acceptance of me makes possible my deepest acceptance of self.

Self-acceptance ultimately implies receiving from the

Lord moment by moment the mystery of myself without distorting or denying who I am and can be. It means living with surprise and disappointment, knowing that I am as capable of the greatest good as I am of the deepest iniquity. Ultimately, for the Christian, attaining a sense of self-worth means experiencing myself as fallible and frail, yet capable with God's grace of transcending my frailty.

Self-acceptance means being open to the wonder the poet Hopkins senses when he says:

> In a flash, at a trumpet crash,
> I am all at once what Christ is, since he was what I am, and
> This Jack, joke, poor potsherd, patch, matchwood, immortal diamond,
> Is immortal diamond.

* * *

Living Up to an Idealized Self-Image

Partly because of childhood background, I have developed the nervous habit of constantly expecting and anticipating disapproval. This habit results in a lack of inner peace, in an inability to be my imperfect self in encounters with others. Is this condition the result of striving to live up to an idealized self-image? What can I do to come to a serene sense of self-acceptance?

* * *

You seem to be caught in a vicious circle. You value a spirit of simplicity, but in trying to achieve this spirit you seem to be observing and analyzing yourself as if you were a specimen under the microscope. You ask, "What can I do?" as if you hope to find some magic formula by which to create inner peace.

In a sense you have already answered your own question. You became aware of an inner disquiet. You found there was nothing you could do to stop being anxious. A stomach full of butterflies cannot be willed away. You tried to come to a deeper understanding of yourself through psychological insights. The disquiet remained, and you are still searching. "What can I do?"

All your efforts at doing so far have been in vain. You have found that nothing you can do will guarantee the change you seek, for self-manipulation and psychological insights in and by themselves cannot produce simplicity.

You have had a tremendous experience, whether you realize it or not. There is nothing you can do. You share the insight and experience of saints and holy men of ages past and present: we stand before the Lord as unprofitable servants. Knowing we are servants, knowing this not just intellectually but experientially, is the beginning of true self-knowledge, the invitation to true self-acceptance.

Your experience of restless searching thus holds the key to the deeper affirmation of self you seek. Only your anxious searching prevented you from seeing the truth St. Augustine told: "My heart is restless until it rests in Thee."

The unique person I am, then, is a response to the mysterious will of the Father for me. I am who I am through the design of the Father's will. This deep sense of self as rooted in the Divine should grant me an experience of genuine self-acceptance.

When I can celebrate my life as gift, not only in the secret depths of my heart but also in union with each person I meet, my new found capacity for self-acceptance will be complemented by quiet joy and a serene sense of personal peace.

As a Christian, moreover, I experience an added dimension of self-acceptance, for I know and believe that as a creature of God I am already accepted, unique and irreplaceable in His eyes.

A loving Father calls me forth from all eternity to be a specific incarnation of His work of redemption. Through the Divine Incarnation, my strengths and weaknesses are drawn into the unfolding mystery of God's redeeming love for me.

Called forth by God, redeemed by Christ, invited to be my deepest self, why then do I find acceptance so difficult?

Perhaps I have confused "acceptance" with "elimination." What I seem to be asking for is not acceptance of myself, with my unique constellation of weaknesses and strengths; rather I seem desirous of eliminating my faults and retaining only my virtues. This willful approach to self hardly sounds accepting.

What I need to do is to adjust my attitude. Acceptance means being able to live with myself as I am, even the self fearful of disapproval and always looking for affirmation.

Living calmly with my limited self—without a frenzied attempt to dispel all faults—can open me to a more realistic appraisal of self. I may see that it is not so much the disapproval of others that has caused me to be so tense as it is my own harsh demand that I act in a perfect way.

At least once in my life, I have probably taken an ungraceful flop. Falling to my knees, I furtively look around and ask, "Did anyone see me or not?" I rise quickly, glance hurriedly down the street, and rush to retrieve the papers I dropped. Three blocks away from the scene, having regained my composure, I attend to my bruised knees and scraped hands. My immediate reaction was not "Did I hurt myself?" but "Did anyone see me fall?"

Clearly when I am not at my best, I feel embarrassed. I dislike losing control of the self-image I project. I want to appear in the right light, to say only the correct thing, and yet I know how uncomfortable it makes me feel to be in the presence of someone who always appears perfect.

It is this compulsion to be perfect that makes me uneasy. I am so busy maintaining my composure that I forget to really listen to myself as a unique source and expression of life.

When I live under the tyranny of an ideal self-image, my acceptance of self depends wholly on acceptance by others.

A teacher, uncertain of self-acceptance, may, for example, spend the greater part of her day looking for signs of approval from her students. Disapproval disheartens her. She needs smiles and looks of acclaim. She depends on loyalty and support at all times. For her identity and acceptance of self lies "out there" in the response of students, on the support of colleagues, on the smiling affirmation of parents.

In Leon Uris' novel *Topaz,* Nicole, the wife of a French intelligence expert, reflects on her broken marriage. She explains that in part at least her actions have been the result of acting out what she thought her husband expected of her. In effect she allowed her life to be lived in light of another's expectation, never honestly responding to what she felt.

I do the same thing every time I tell myself "they" won't like what I am doing or "they" will never think this is a good idea. I allow the anonymous "they" to run my life.

How can I shift the center of acceptance from "out there" to "within"? What are the dynamics of an acceptance of self rooted in me as I am and not dependent on what I or others think I should be?

My feelings, likes and dislikes, needs and desires, thoughts and opinions—all the factors past and present that affect me as a person—influence the way in which I experience and respond to each situation. No other person can have exactly the same responses as I.

It follows from this that I can respect, trust, and accept

the self that is revealed to me in the uniqueness of my responses. I do not need to construct an ideal image based on what I think others are expecting or demanding of me.

My true self-image is based on the person I have become in response to the life I have lived and am living. The more I become myself, the more necessary it may be to establish new goals. Despite the risk involved, the struggle to be myself is worth the effort, especially when it leads me to the Source of my strength.

Without this sense of self as emerging from the Sacred, the inner acceptance I wish to attain may never occur. To be at peace with myself, I have to be able to laugh at my incongruities. My life is bound to include periods of self-doubt, depression, and possibly even despair. Such signs of fallibility are what bind me to the rest of mankind.

These foibles are also the entrance ways by which I allow God to come into my life. For if I were not imperfect and sinful, I would have no need of a Redeemer.

* * *

Relying on External Forms of Devotionalism and Behaviorism

As a religious, I find it is only too easy to rely heavily on external forms of devotionalism and behaviorism. Such reliance on the external gives me a false sense of security and seems to be an obstacle to self-acceptance.

* * *

The change from an exclusively behavioristic style of life to personal religious living rests ultimately with you as a person. Your whole way of being—your thoughts, emotions, and values—needs to be reawakened.

An encrustation of external modes of comportment may have almost suffocated the Spirit within you. The call to reawakening may come to you gently or in a sudden moment of clarity. Frequently, this call for deepening comes during a time of personal crisis when ambitions and projects appear meaningless, when you are filled with a boredom close to despair. Stripped of all props, you dare to ask, "Where am I going?"

When you reach this crucial phase of your spiritual unfolding, you can do little more than create conditions favorable for the awakening of the Spirit. You cannot force this enlightenment to occur. You can only clear the tangled weeds of your life so that God may walk in the clearing.

It may comfort you to know that this problem is not yours alone. Anyone who relies mainly on external forms of devotionalism and behaviorism needs some help in coming to self-awareness and self acceptance.

To solve this problem, my first inclination may be to look for a technique. *If only* I could find the right combination of techniques, *then* I could increase my self-awareness. So the reasoning goes, but the situation is more complex than this.

Like other members of contemporary society, I live by certain behavioristic codes emerging from the general aura of technique and problem-solving in which we live. The trouble is that I carry these behavioristic codes, suitable for living in society, to my personal life. Instead of becoming more human, more personally responsible for the quality of my relation to self, situation and others, I tend to look for lasting solutions to life problems in impersonal techniques.

There are many such techniques available at the moment. They range from some types of sensitivity training to self-discovery trips via hallucinogenic drugs.

While under certain conditions, and in response to well-defined needs, such techniques may promote a degree of self-awareness, they are not an ultimate solution. Moreover, they leave untouched the initial problem—that of using problem-solving techniques for responding to the fundamental mystery of life.

I cannot live on the level of problem-solving technique alone. The self-awareness that results from such procedures is limited and can be crippling in its effects, both physically and emotionally.

Awareness of self calls for the freedom to respond to each situation uniquely. Becoming a slave to certain psychological or chemical techniques is not the answer. If I begin to solve essentially self-level difficulties by means of mere ego-techniques, there is little chance of genuine growth taking place.

In other words, self-awareness, which is not accomplished in freedom, may only be another form of behaviorism. New techniques replace the old. For former ways of feeling secure, I substitute new ways which are equally false.

What if I should discover that my spirituality is only a matter of devotionalistic and behavioristic practices. Clearly I need to reexamine my values and style of living. The danger to guard against is that I do not substitute a new form of "in" behavior for an old style of "out" behavior. Were I to do this, I would still be in the mold of religious behaviorism.

My whole approach to this problem has to be tempered by a respectful love for self and others. If my concern is genuine, I can affirm what is positive in my devotional life. A patient attitude may give me the strength I need to look again at the obstacles to religious presence a life of false security can bring.

Especially today there are historical reasons why I would seek for such security. In ages past, man rose painfully and slowly to greater realization of his unique potential for personal and spiritual growth. Development was so gradual that successive generations did not differ much in their view of life and reality.

Since the Renaissance, however, human development has progressed at an accelerating pace which in our day reaches a dizzying tempo. What before would have taken hundreds of years to accomplish may now be done in a few.

In most cases, my ability to adapt is not able to keep up with the rapid explosion of my culture. More and more developments seem to pass me by. I feel increasingly insecure. Little wonder that I try to hold on frantically to a style of living that makes me feel at least externally safe.

Again I ought not to blame myself for failing to keep up with the grueling pace of development. I have to do the best I can with what I have been given during my own years of religious formation. If I am able to personalize my religious practices, no matter how dated they may be, I can enjoy the sense of security they bring.

Gradually, with much patience and respect, I may attempt to broaden my horizon. If, however, I do not wish to grow in a certain direction, then arguments to the contrary are of little avail.

What to another may look like an outdated devotional practice may really mean something in my life of prayer. If I feel happy and comfortable praying this way, I should not force myself to change merely for the sake of change. The paths to God are many; no generation can traverse or exhaust them all.

Times change but the goal of spiritual unfolding remains the same: the reality of the Divine has to so permeate my life that there can be no separation between outward expression and inward belief. The permanence of the Holy must radiate in every temporary activity. The sense of the numinous should be felt in every manifestation of life and labor.

I must be transformed inwardly by my loving presence to God. This attitude of devotion need not always be expressed in outward forms of prayer but when the occasion for formal prayer arises I should respond spontaneously and personally. I do not force myself to fit into any preconceived notion of what prayer should be; I simply pray.

I place myself before God as the person I am. I ask nothing more than to become an embodiment of His love. I shun the road of impersonal pietistic devotionalism. I avoid falling into a pattern of prayer that may never be personalized. Otherwise prayer, which should bring me to life, becomes personally deadening.

True prayer is a path to self-awareness and self-acceptance. Whether mine is a call for help in an agonizing moment of terror or a spontaneous burst of gratitude for another perfect day, the value of prayer is undeniable.

To return to true devotion and prayer from mere patterns of devotionalism and piety is the responsibility of every religious person and especially of those who have chosen the consecrated life. As one spiritual master reminds us, "God hath not given us a greater argument of His willingness to have us saved, and of our unwillingness to accept it, His goodness and our gracelessness, His infinite condescension and our carelessness and folly, than by rewarding so easy a duty with so great blessings."

QUESTIONS AND ANSWERS

on

III. PERMANENT COMMITMENT

Making a Permanent Commitment

* * *

Making A Permanent Commitment

Many today question the advisability of making a permanent commitment. Man, they say, is dynamic and open. Why must he choose a fundamental life form? He should be ready to meet the new commitments growth and discovery might bring. He should be open to all life forms and find meaning in them. How does one who believes in permanent commitment respond to this kind of thinking?

* * *

But the serpent said to the woman: "You certainly will not die! No, God knows well that the moment you eat of it you will be like gods, who know what is good and what is bad."

Genesis 3:4-5

The desire to be like gods—this is what prompts man's vain yearning to be open to all that is. This desire is not foreign to human nature. I have within my finiteness something of the infinite. As a spirit-self, I am openness to all that is, but because of my body, I am situated in time and space. Being in a body determines the way my potential openness will be lived out.

If I am fixing a sandwich in the kitchen, I cannot be sunbathing in the backyard. If I am meeting someone in town for dinner at 6:15, I cannot meet my friend's plane at 6:20. My body locates me in space and time. It limits my range of possibilities. I must choose to be in the kitchen or in the yard.

I might want to be scholar, sculptor, and seaman, but space and time do not permit me to be excellent in all three of these endeavors at once. I have to choose which one I want to excell in and then devote myself to it wholeheartedly.

Each choice I make limits me; at the same time new possibilities open up as well. I discover talents I did not know I had. Opportunities that never would have been mine are there for the taking.

Reading a good book determines the way I will spend my time while revealing new insights that may influence my living in days to come.

Living within these limits and the possibilities they provide I continue to grow and become. Limitation is thus the price of humanness. When I try to escape my limits—to be like the gods—I not only fail to be divine; I cease to live a fully human life.

Commitment does not mean that growth ceases. What it does imply is a choice.

In adolescence many worlds open before me. Commitment, I think, is submission. Others will have claims on me and claims are too confining. I want to be free. I want to take life as it comes—ready for everything and anything. Never stopping or settling down. Always on the go. Life is a field of beautiful daffodils—I want them all; why should I choose one?

In adolescence the field seems infinite but, as I grow, I start to look at particular daffodils. Some are lovely and become even lovelier; others lose their attractiveness and seem out of tune with my personal likes and dislikes. I experience myself as limited. I find that I am able to gather in but a few of the daffodils I would like to keep.

As I move from adolescence to adulthood, I realize that I cannot be and do and have everything. I must make a choice, assume responsibility, select a definite way of life by which to gather together the diffused fragments of my self discovered thus far. This choice involves risk.

I experience myself torn in different directions by inner and outer forces. I suffer from feelings of disunity and fragmentation, coupled with a relentless search for some foundation on which to build my selfhood. The risk of commitment is in venturing my all, but the failure to do so may mean a wasted life.

In order to bear fruit, my nature requires the rooting characteristic of permanent commitment. Such commitment is not merely advisable; it is a necessity. If there is no order or direction in my life, growth can be as haphazard and unhealthy as the erratic multiplication of cancer cells.

By uttering the irrevocable *yes* of total commitment, I lay the foundation for healthy growth. I can spend years saying maybe or not yet to life but the avoidance of commitment only enfeebles my spirit. With no light to guide me, my life may end in inner emptiness, frustration, and perhaps despair.

The kind of commitment that demands unconditional surrender of self in love to another human being in marriage or to God as a celibate in the world or to Him through the vows of religious life is always made in partial darkness. By entering deeply into myself, I try to discern the will of God for me. I sense that my life is moving in a coherent direction. I approach a decision. My life begins to fall into place. In some indescribable way, I sense that God is guiding my relationship to Him.

The call to a life form is experienced as a gift from God received in the darkness of faith. This call may be to a life consecrated exclusively to Him. I know God and I know my call—not with scientific accuracy, not as I know a blueprint or a road map, but as I know a person.

In one sense I can say I have chosen my religious life but in another sense I have been chosen as well.

Under the guidance of a master of religious living, this

call is made concrete by a mature, definite, and personal commitment of myself to God through final vows.

Once I commit myself to a specific life form—married, single or religious—I do not cease committing myself. Commitment demands more than legal fulfillment of the terms of my promise. It calls for a faithfulness to the deep reasons that prompted me to make this commitment in the first place.

I have to remain faithful to my original motivation, even in moments of doubt and dismay. My choice of new commitments has to be integrated within my fundamental life orientation.

When I marry, marital love for a woman besides my wife is for me out of the question but love for my wife becomes deeper as a result.

When I choose the religious life, exclusive love for a partner of the opposite sex is no longer possible, but this celibate mode frees me for a deepening awareness of God as the center of my life and of my responsibility to bring the good news of His love to others in the culture.

Love grows in the act of caring; hope in being faithful day by day; and trust in renewing the kind of fidelity I originally chose to live.

Choosing a life form thus gives my life direction and purpose and provides a setting within which individual options acquire an overall unified and coherent meaning. Form is the principle that gives unity to the whole. This unity is broken if I live half in and half out of my life form.

For example, externally I may be living as a religious but internally my imagination, feelings, perceptions are fed by the fantasy of what it would be like to be a wife and mother. I am not a wife and mother; neither am I a religious. I simply go through the motions of the external structure of religious life while living in the aura of a fantasized married life.

In the name of openness, I absorb the ideas of others without critically evaluating them. One opinion becomes as good as the next. Soon this juggling of opinions begins to erode values on which I have based my life: like the value of permanent commitment to Christ in religious community. Juggling theories then becomes a personally dangerous game.

Is it possible that I have mistaken a call and chosen the wrong life form? This is possible, of course, but a change of life form should not be taken lightly. Change must not be confused with the prevalent desire to try everything out.

A committed life is never a guarantee that I will be freed from anxiety, frustration, unsureness. These are the inevitable hardships that will be experienced in any life form. Indeed I can hardly claim to have lived if I have not met life's sufferings as well as its joys.

Unwillingness to root myself in one or the other life form may be fascinating for a while—since it carries the illusion of freedom, but it is only a kind of irresponsibility.

Remember Faust. He sells his soul to the devil for the power to be what he wishes. At one time he is an artist, at another the husband of Helen of Troy, later a general, an engineer, a colonizer, an empire builder. The price of this openness is Faust's soul.

On the other hand, when I shape my integrity, aspirations, hopes, fears, joys and talents according to a specific life form, I discover my unique personality while contributing in a creative way to the world around me.

I see that it is fruitless to envision a life of unlimited openness but most fruitful to live open within limits.

QUESTIONS AND ANSWERS

on

IV. PRAYER

To Whom Am I Listening? God or Myself

Reflection vs. Introspection

Play and Prayer

Neglecting Prayer

Aim of Meditation

Appraisal of the Spirit

* * *

To Whom Am I Listening? God or Myself

I try to meditate, but all I seem to accomplish is talking to myself. It is so easy to deceive myself into thinking I am listening to the Will of God, when all I am actually listening to is my egotistical self. How can I tell the difference?

* * *

Coming in from the rush of school activities, breathing heavily, I sit down in chapel. This is the time I have set aside for prayer. I try to shift my mind and body from scheduled class time to the unscheduled experience of prayer. I begin to probe various avenues of thought.

Soon I notice that the external quiet of the chapel is in sharp contrast to the noise of my inner activity. What is meant to be a time of contemplation, of recollected listening to the Lord, becomes just another instance of busy listening to myself.

Students with problems, deadlines, anxiety-provoking headlines, headaches, phone calls, unpaid bills, misunderstandings with friends and co-workers, personal ups and downs—all seem to crowd into my meditation despite my efforts to pay exclusive attention to prayer. It seems as if I spend most of the time talking to myself about all these people and events.

The encounters of the day crowd in and demand my attention even more during reflective moments. How am I supposed to pray? Why do I feel like such a scatter-brain? What's wrong with my powers of concentration?

This experience is familiar to anyone who tries to turn wholly to God in times of prayer. It would be a mistake to imagine that I could bypass my ego-centered self and approach God directly on a purely spiritual plane.

I cannot leave my daily activities outside the chapel door and rise to the level of pure spirit as soon as I cross the threshold. I bring my whole world with me when I enter into dialogue with God. I must start from where I am, not from where I would like to be. Otherwise I am in danger of deceiving myself.

Any encounter, including prayer, involves the meeting of two persons. I must first become present to my own self as grounded in a particular life situation. Only then can I open myself to the presence of God and enter into a meaningful relationship with Him.

Let's say I have had an exhausting, disappointing, or fruitful day. Then this day is my starting point for meeting God. I must be in touch with myself and my lived situation if my prayer is going to be the means by which I unite my whole life to the will of God for me.

What counts is not how well I measure up to my expectations of grandeur and success but whether I am in tune with God's plan for me. My concern then shifts from self in isolation to whatever it is that prevents me from giving myself more fully to the One in whom I live and move and have my being.

One barrier to prayer may be the functional culture in which I live. In a world of doing, it is common to take a project-like approach to reality. The "teacher me" plans lessons. The "homemaker me" purchases the week's groceries. The "bookkeeper me" figures out the monthly accounts. I may carry this same attitude of managing into prayer. I want to "do" my prayers well and even "manage" God.

In my desire to be near Him, I may be drawn to new methods and techniques of praying. I may feel that with sufficient research, study and effort, I can attain the aim I set out to accomplish. My limits are inevitably exposed when I attempt to control and regulate my approach to God or His approach to me.

In true prayer my manipulative self has to recede to the background. Because prayer is a gift, I allow God to be for me. I take the humble stance of receiver. Lovingly, quietly, waiting in an attitude of expectancy and receptivity, I open myself to God. I am present to Him. I allow myself to be touched and moved by Him on every level of my being. I realize painfully that contemplation is not produced by a method of prayer, a psychological technique, an intellectual process.

Contemplation is a gift of grace, not attained by my efforts alone. Day after day I come to God with an attitude of openness and expectation. There may be lengthy times of waiting in silence. The anguish of this waiting often draws me to fill up the silence with busy speech or to take flight in fantasy.

I soon discover that neither reasoning nor questioning bring me the certitude of His presence. All I can do is return daily and say with the psalmist, ". . . my soul longs for you, O God" (Psalm 42). With faith, patience and humility, I follow what seems to be a dark and lonely path to God. And because His grace is boundless, I may be opened to Him when I least suspect it, seeing His presence everywhere and in all things.

On the other hand, if I leave prayer restless and frustrated, it may be because I have only gone to the chapel to seek an instant solution to spiritual problems. Prayer should ready me to accept life as it presents itself. Even if it does not solve particular problems, somehow I can be reconciled to God's will.

True prayer begins when I unite my will to the will of the Father whose presence I seek to embody in my limited life situation. Rather than trying to split the day into active moments and contemplative ones, I may find it more realistic to look into the "active me" during frequent brief moments of meditation.

What does today mean for me in relation to the Spirit in whom all men are one? Does my behavior reflect an attitude of trust in the Lord? Do I remain mindful of the deeper reality of Christian unity in the midst of pressured moments and personality conflicts?

Formal periods of meditation on the meaning of my spiritual life become more satisfying if I am able to reflect momentarily on the meaning of single moments many times during the day. To return to the center of my Christian motivation as frequently as I can benefits me in two ways. It can prevent me from living a fragmented, exhausting and merely task-oriented existence. And such frequent turning inward makes it easier for me to gather myself before God when the time does come for recollection.

* * *

Reflection vs. Introspection

Many people confuse reflection with being turned in upon themselves (introspection). Some clarification of the difference might help me to know a little more about the necessity and how of dwelling and meditative reflection in tune with daily life.

* * *

Think of a situation in which you argued with someone. Opinions clash. Tempers flare up. When the argument is over you walk away in a flurry of irritation.

If your nature tends to be introspective, you may churn the situation and your feelings over again and again. You analyze every move. You think your opponent does not like you. She will not accept your ideas. Maybe she is trying to get even with you for something. Or you may try to figure out why you got furious with her. Maybe she reminds you of your dominating mother or a teacher you didn't like in school.

This kind of circular thinking fosters introspection. I go around inside myself getting nowhere. I merely add fuel to my passion and stir up more anger and resentment. I'm like a cat chasing its tail, meeting myself coming and going. This approach leads to a dead end. I cannot become prayerful merely by analyzing my problems and feelings.

If I dwell on the same situation in meditative reflection, my concern becomes the Divine Will and not who was right or wrong. I ask what this particular situation tells me about myself that either hinders or enhances my compliance with the Divine Will. Perhaps my pride was hurt because my ideas were not accepted. Maybe I have to struggle with a temper that flares up when things don't go my way.

In meditative reflection I cease trying to figure out why I feel angry or proud; I simply acknowledge who I am here and now and try to see the message of the Divine speaking through this incident. I draw closer to Him by letting go of my ideas and self-sufficiency, by humbly submitting to a situation I cannot change, even though I may still suffer hurt feelings.

Dwelling and meditative reflection describe an approach to prayer that places me in a context much wider than my isolated self. I see myself against the background of events, people, and things, of historical and cultural situations, of the broad universe of natural forms that both hide and reveal the presence of the Divine. And all of these elements form the warp and woof of my existence and are permeated by the omnipresent Divine Will of the Father.

When I dwell in this context in moments of prayer, I experience the wholeness and integrity of my being as coming forth in love from the Father, redeemed by the Son, interiorly led by the Spirit.

Introspection by contrast cuts my inner life off from this wider horizon. I focus on isolated emotions and feelings in the hope of finding personal integration. The effort is futile. For the limitations I have imposed on my horizon frustrate my quest from the start.

Preoccupied with this or that task or project, I may at times become unduly agitated with people, with the world, with myself. I live my days one after the other in an automatic, uncritical fashion. I may "make meditation" on Scripture or one of the spiritual writers but I omit reflection on my daily life in the light of the Divine Will. I fail to "shake out the pieces" in meditative fashion to see if I have "practiced the truth in love." My prayer life then becomes detached and free-floating; it has little or no connection with my everyday actions.

In the midst of such turmoil I must listen to my tired, agitated self. This feeling is the way reality is revealing itself to me. I need to set aside moments for meditative reflection so that I can realize more fully the sense of God alive and working in me however my feeling state. When I reflect on my joys, disappointments, frustrations, and unexpected graces as coming from and pointing to the mysterious, unspeakable love of God, I practice the art of meditative reflection.

Meditative reflection does not suggest a turning in on myself in a process of introspective scrutiny. Neither is it an examination of conscience done in the same way I inspect clothes that are soiled and need to be washed. Meditative reflection is the way by which I seek to be in touch with God, to see the events of my daily life in light of His will.

Seeing the need I have for dwelling and meditative reflection is not enough. Through Scripture, I am assured of the presence of God within me. A recurring theme of St. John's is: I know I am living in Him and He is living in me because He lets me share His spirit. St. Paul encourages us "to live in Christ Jesus the Lord, in the spirit in which you received Him. Be rooted in Him, growing ever stronger in faith, as you were taught, and overflowing with gratitude" (Colossians 2:6-7).

As I center myself on these thoughts, I may begin to see my life in a new light. I am better able to dispose myself to God's presence within me. I see more clearly that I do not live my life in isolation. With my fellow men, I participate in God's love, in the goodness and beauty of his creation.

Meditation is my quiet effort to be mindful of God who permeates and transcends my ordinary day to day life. At times, I know I am called to speak with Him face to face, as a man speaks with his friend. So I meditate. I remember His presence, His meaning, and the influence of His faithful love in my life. I meditate because I am loved and want to love in return.

True love never forgets. It clings to the remembrance of the Beloved. Such love is the abiding, inspiring source of meditation. The "how" of meditation comes naturally to one who loves.

Love seeking mindfulness listens to the voice of the Beloved and to the intimations of His presence in the now moment. Love is an empty vessel waiting to be filled. Love seeks and discovers the presence of God through listening to His word. Prayer is speaking to Him who has first addressed us.

Listening, responding, being with the Source and Goal of my life are all moments in meditative experience. I can never be told precisely "how" to live these moments. Whether they are interwoven throughout the whole of daily life or are experienced during the special time reserved for prayer, they are always moments that express the surprise and secrecy of love.

* * *

Play and Prayer

In what way can play time be integrated wisely and
wholesomely with prayer time?

* * *

"A stereotyped but unconscious despair is concealed
even under what are called the games and amusements of
mankind. There is no play in them, for this comes after
work. But it is characteristic of wisdom not to do desperate
things."

Over one hundred years ago Thoreau wrote these words
while at Walden Pond. It is frightening that things have
changed so little in all that time.

Thoreau was mindful of the encroaching forces of
materialism, individualism, and industrialization. We are
grappling with the problems created by advanced
technology and the seeming triumph of utilitarian values.

When I am not busy, I feel guilty. I am torn between
hours spent efficiently organizing my life and the minutes I
set aside to "waste" time. Shaped and formed by a
technological culture that measures time in terms of money
or goods, I hesitate to play. When I finish playing, "I have
nothing to show for it." Unconsciously I tend to value
material gain more than hidden spiritual values. This
pervasive attitude lessens the possibility of play.

A steady tension exists between needing and liking my
work and the danger of allowing it to dominate my life.
Even when I engage in recreation, I may do so in order to
function more effectively in work. I may sadly regard
recreation as a waste of time and so devise ways of relaxing
while washing the car or engaging in strenuous exercise

Work becomes deadly serious business for me. It surpasses all other dimensions of life and may exclude the possibility of a playful attitude. Recreation seems meaningless if not linked to work. Prayer appears unproductive compared to the results of a full day's receipts.

I need to distance myself from my work long enough to see the proper place of service in the totality of my life. At first this distancing may engender anxiety. Having identified living and working, I may no longer feel comfortable unless I am actively engaged.

The experience of guilt does not disappear merely when I'm told that play is not a waste of time. Guilt feelings are especially prevalent in a productive society and may remain with me even if I concede that play is a positively healthful experience.

Through repeated efforts, accompanied perhaps by supportive encouragement from someone who understands the value of play, I may begin to appreciate the need for recreation to foster the religious values in which I want to ground my life.

Strained efforts to play are not the answer either. Happy, informal, spontaneous presence to reality will most likely emerge when I unlearn compulsive habits of control. Understanding some of the unconscious motives that hinder playfulness and prayer may also help.

If I find it difficult to play, this may be due to a strain of negativity running through my life. Little things irritate me. I complain from day to day about other people and the lazy lives they lead. I enjoy tearing down structure and institutions but am loathe to suggest ways to rebuild them. I am prompt to point out the faults of my neighbor but rather reticent about my own failings.

Perhaps I should feel guilty not because I have done too little but because I have tried to do too much. Unlike the poet, I have been so busy that I have lost my playful sense of wonder. I have forgotten to accept myself as I am and have been driven to exhaustion by futile strivings to be someone else. That is why I cannot pray, for prayer involves a turning of my whole being toward the Lord.

To prevent displacement of life by labor is a challenge facing all of us in cont~mporary society. Religious especially are called to point the way toward the deepest meaning of life which lies beyond one's capacity to produce goods and services. Work can be a path to the Lord but it can also distract me from His presence.

As a Christian the first meaning of my commitment is to radiate the love of the Lord in and through my life style. I should strive to live this love in a personal way so that my participation in the culture points toward its transcendent meaning.

I must also organize my time to include moments of not doing and develop in these a sense of play. Eventually I may begin to "play" at my work. This relaxed attitude of responsible carefreeness as opposed to compulsive preoccupation is not easy to attain.

Enjoyment comes from doing the best I can without the anxious feeling that I must do everything or be dubbed a failure.

Reserving time for living the "inactivity" of recreation gives me the peace of mind I need to respond fully to the moment. I forget about what should be done, and what more I can do, and concentrate on doing my best now.

I perceive with clarity that living is not measured by how much I have done but by the way in which my endeavors embody the love of the Lord.

I enter wholeheartedly into the experience of enjoying a good book, going to the theater, listening to music, strolling in the park, lying in the sun.

A capacity for non-compulsive play may be an opening to the experience of prayerful presence. There is no substitute for prayer if I would live my life to the full and not despair at its passing. This awareness should prompt me to develop a leisurely attitude of inner "letting go." Only when I let go of my ego life may I make room for the Spirit to enter in.

* * *

Neglecting Prayer

A new freedom has entered religious life regarding prayer. Much good has resulted from this. The bad feature seems to be that some put their prayer life last, at times neglecting it altogether. I would like to know how to respond to this matter without encroaching on another's personal freedom.

* * *

I may see another neglecting prayer and remind her of this, but I must first make sure that true concern is motivating me to speak. If my words merely cloak anger or resentment, she will sense my hostility and react in kind. She may feel I am imposing my values on her and resist my reminders all the more.

A second possibility is to say little or nothing, pretending to be oblivious to the situation. Silence in this case may only mean "I don't really care about you."

On the other hand, if I am caring and she is open, genuine communication may be possible. Even though she may be hurt initially by what I say, nonetheless, sensing my concern for her, she may tell me why she does not want to pray. Perhaps she feels our community prayer has become trite and repetitious. In reacting to this deficiency, she may have mistakenly dismissed prayer completely. Whatever the difficulty is, we can learn from one another if we meet on a person to person basis.

The other may turn a deaf ear to my concern. This is an

ever present risk. The more I care, the deeper I am open to pain. In the last analysis I can only approach the other knowing full well that she has the freedom to accept or reject my offer to help.

Experiencing the value of prayer in my life, it is understandable that I wish to share this value with others. However, I must not forget each person's unique pace and predisposition. Attempting to impress my values upon one who is not open to impression is an imposition on my part. I may only succeed in impressing him negatively if I am not more careful.

If the apparent absence of prayer in the life of a person causes me worry, perhaps the best thing I can do is to remain faithful to prayer in my own life. My fidelity may then lead the other by contrast to ask what is missing in her life.

Christ spoke little about prayer in public, but He prayed a great deal. When His disciples came to Him and asked, "Lord, teach us to pray" (Luke 11:1), they had been made ready for prayer by His example.

The fact that I am always present in chapel will not impress anyone unless the other senses in daily contact with me the fruits of such discipline. "You can tell a tree by its fruit" (Matthew 7:20). If there is a quiet serenity in my deepest self and a respectful openness to the other's uniqueness, he may recognize my care as genuine.

I need not be concerned about whether the other perceives me as prayerful or not. If I am truly present to the Lord in times of prayer, this presence will overflow into daily life. In fact, the less conscious I am of myself and my appearance, the more I will be respectfully present to the other. In my respect I may feel the responsibility to admonish him.

I may risk such a reproof provided I am willing to take the consequences of what might result. He may have more deep seated problems than his seeming lack of desire for prayer. If I open up these problems, I must be willing to see to it that this person receives the help he needs to work them through. Even if I cannot help him directly, I must give him support and understanding when he seeks help elsewhere.

If I sense that an admonition would not be well taken or if I cannot assume responsibility for what might result, I ought simply to go on with my own sincere living of religious values. I do so not in a spirit of "I'll mind my business and you do the same." Rather I remain genuinely open for the moment when the other reaches out to seek my advice and I am prepared to take the risk of speaking to him.

Without prayer, a Christian eventually discovers that he has cut his own life-lines. Neglect of prayer is analogous to a power failure. When I cease to draw strength and light from God in prayer, I may experience insecurity and lack of direction in my life. My work may miss inspiration with the result that school or hospital duties become dull routine.

Without the light shed by nearness to Christ, I may at most grope along, hoping through my own efforts to achieve some measure of fulfillment.

Other sisters might caution me about the folly of neglecting prayer. Persons whom I respect and trust may manifest concern for my spiritual life. Their words make good sense, but what if I counter them with the falsehood, "My work is my prayer." What then?

Perhaps only painful, personal experience of my own insufficiency will again bring me to my knees before God. Perhaps I have to learn the hard way that trying to live the religious life without a deepening relation to Christ is as risky as driving alone in the dark with no traffic signs to illumine obstacles or to warn me of approaching intersections.

Prayer may only become a felt necessity for me when in my own weakness I experience my dependency on Christ. Witness what happened to Peter. (Luke 5:1-11) An expert fisherman, he had been on the lake all night and caught nothing. At daybreak, Christ called to him from the shore to cast his net to the right side; immediately a miraculous catch flooded the nets. Christ taught Peter humility and dependence by allowing him to experience personal inadequacy in the trade where he was considered master. This humbling experience taught Peter much more than he might have understood from a sermon or a bit of advice. Face to face with his own finiteness, Peter realized his personal helplessness without the Lord.

If I have been neglecting prayer, often only a sense of my nothingness leads me to prayerful surrender to His allness.

* * *

Aim of Meditation

If the main aim of meditation is to develop an all day long inner spirit of recollection, why is it necessary to spend some time each day in formal meditation. Cannot an in depth discussion with a friend be meditation?

* * *

Countless ideas, attitudes, people, and things vie for my attention. It is impossible to give all equal time. Meditation helps me to see what aids my direction in life and to reject what diffuses this purpose.

Such acceptance and rejection may also take place in discussion with a friend. Discussion, if it is deep, also helps to direct my life.

Nonetheless, discussion with a friend cannot replace inner silence, the gathering of forces, and the continuous initiative to turn to God required in meditation. This is neither to deny the value of discussion nor to glorify recollection; it is merely to distinguish between two unique and necessary ways of being.

To allow things, events, and people to speak to me of God necessitates a time for renewing and deepening my relationship with the Divine. As in any interpersonal relationship, I must have time to be alone with the Other. The length of time may vary but what matters is that through it our relationship is deepened.

Constant revitalization is needed if my daily life is to be permeated by presence to God. I may gain new insights and perspectives through discussions with a friend. These may supplement but can never substitute for the time necessary for being alone with God.

A friend may experience the same event as me but find a meaning within it which differs from mine. The Holy Spirit speaks uniquely to each of us.

The primary goal of meditation is personal union between God and the soul. Meditation is a communication between persons who wish to know each other more intimately. How does such communion come about?

Because I am human, my relationship with a person cannot develop in a vacuum. Our friendship might disappear if we restricted ourselves to a few words and a vague feeling of warmth. Love would progressively become more diffuse and in time evaporate simply because we lacked sufficient contact.

Just as friends find it necessary to spend time together, after being alone, so a person who has consecrated her life to God finds it necessary to be alone with Him. She also grows in love by her labors for Him, but it is only in her intimate meetings that she can know and love Him more fully.

As she speaks to Him of her daily concerns and listens to

His counsel, she finds the strength and understanding she needs. As she ponders in His presence the continual revelation He has left her in the Gospels, she becomes aware of what she can do to please Him.

The more I experience prayer as personal communion with God, the clearer I see that it can never be encapsulated within a half-hour interval or a few succinct phrases. At the same time, I realize that I stand in God's presence as a human person. It would be rash to imagine I could bypass my humanity in my search for God.

Meditation may be aimed at attaining an all day long inner spirit of recollection, but its principle concern is to deepen the relationship between God and myself.

Being with others ought not to exclude my being alone. Rather it is in the interaction of solitude and communion that I can discover one main rhythm of religious life.

Discussion with a friend implies my ability to live on both of these levels. Communion without solitude is empty; solitude without communion could lead to unhealthy isolation. Living the rhythm of solitude and communion cannot be accomplished if I am constantly doing and talking. Nor can I explicitly reflect on my own life while explicitly being with the other. I have to take time out to recollect myself in Christ.

Prayer is an openness and a listening more than a speaking. It is an event which takes place between man and God. Prayer begins in the individual soul which is readied by silence and recollection to hear God speak and willing to respond to His voice in faith and love.

Neglect of meditative prayer may create a gap between me and God with the eventual loss on my part of a sense of His presence.

Spiritual growth requires periods of devout prayer. I need not be rigid about the exact time, place or manner of praying, but it is perhaps a wise concession to human frailty to determine a certain time each day for this loving engagement.

In prayerful listening, I open myself to greater enlightenment, allowing Christ to lead me to the Father. This openness is possible only if I can for some moments sufficiently distance myself from other matters and turn my thoughts to the presence of God within me.

Discussion with a friend can at times help me to recollect and center scattered psychic forces, but this is simply a prelude to personal prayer. After such interpersonal dialogues, if I am sincere in my desire to deepen loving union with God, I must be willing to withdraw from others for a while to listen to Him alone in a quiet meditation that allows God to have the last word.

* * *

Appraisal of the Spirit

We listen to the Spirit in silence, but many "spirits" are clamoring to be heard—all under the guise of the good. How do we recognize (appraise) the true Spirit?

* * *

Like any art, appraisal of spirits requires disciplined openness and patient waiting. If I am a concert pianist, my art has demanded years of disciplined and patient openness to my instructor, the musical scores, my own skills and weaknesses, the audience for whom I perform.

In the art of spiritual appraisal, I also need to be a "disciplined openness" to certain kinds of norms. To appraise whether I am moved by the Spirit of God or by a spirit of self-seeking, I need to enter into dialogue with myself, with the Gospel, with the teaching Church.

God speaks through my own person as I am in this situation. I have to listen to myself—to the gift of my own nature and to the gifts of God's grace in my life. Does what I feel moved to do "by the Spirit" really express my God-given uniqueness? If there is a harmony between who I am and what I feel moved to do, I will feel at one with myself and others. I will experience peace as I follow the attraction of the Spirit, even though this attraction may call me into the midst of conflict.

Secondly, I listen to the Gospel, especially to the heart of the Gospel, which is the cross of Christ. The cross is the great crisis point of all human life. "Crisis" implies judgment. Therefore, the cross must be the central norm of judgment in appraising what spirit moves me. Does what I am moved to do somehow conform me to Christ and to the mystery of His cross? Does it move me to peaceful surrender to the Father? Does it move me beyond my own little world into more authentic concern for others?

Finally, I listen to the teaching of the Church. There is no contradiction between the Spirit who governs and directs me and the Spirit who guides the Church. If what I am moved to do is in accord with the teaching Church, then it more likely is truly from the Spirit who animates my life and the life of the whole Body of Christ.

If I am fortunate, I may have a living expression of the teaching Church in the person of a good spiritual director. In candid openness to him, my instructor and guide in the ways of the Spirit, I may slowly learn to live as the "tuning fork" of God and thus sound to the world the unique melody I am.

How do I prepare myself for listening to the Spirit?

Initially a quieting has to take place in me. It is relatively easy to remove myself from external sources that elicit my attention. I can turn off the TV, put aside the newspaper, find a spot where I can be alone.

I soon discover that the clamoring was not merely external to myself. I find myself arguing inwardly over conflicting claims. This inner disquiet may absorb my attention so much that it prevents an inner quiet wherein the Spirit can speak and be heard.

Many things in my life jolt me, cause me to be confused, and perhaps to lose my sense of direction. Many voices are crying to be heard. I realize that books, lectures, and opinions of others have an important place in my life but, in our over-stimulated world, these things are hammering at me from so many different directions that I am confused. To whom should I listen? What should I do?

The first thing is to stop searching frantically. If I dwell reflectively on who I am and where I am going, perhaps in the silence of my soul I shall hear the will of God being made known to me a little at a time, situation by situation.

When I am in touch with what is real for me, I may be able to open myself to the "prophetic" voices around me, sift out what is good and meaningful for me as a religious person, and discard what appears to be harmful to my unique unfolding.

In seeking to know the ways of the Spirit, I can also rely on my community's wisdom. A basic readiness for the Spirit's disclosure is achieved when I and others have prayed alone and studied seriously. Persons who have opened themselves to the Spirit can trust in His guiding their community. The Lord has given His assurance for this: "Where two or three are gathered in my name, there am I in their midst" (Matthew 18:20).

Because I am not traveling through life alone but am going to God with the countless other unique persons I meet, I realize that some of the voices are meant for them and not necessarily for me. I am aware, too, that because I am human, I shall make mistakes in choosing what is best for me.

Though I may periodically lose my sense of direction and take a more roundabout way to God, I ought to remember that because the Kingdom of God is within me, I am already the possessor of that for which I search.

The Spirit continues to speak to me in the limited words of others and even when He speaks the perfect truth in the core of my life, He may be imperfectly heard by me. I must risk acting on this imperfect knowledge. Hearing the confusion of all partial truths, considering the way my motives and onesidedness color the situation, I choose what I sense is best. I need not add to the confusion by tensely fearing that I will make the wrong choice. God does not reject me for my hearing imperfectly but incorporates my mistake into His plan.

QUESTIONS AND ANSWERS

on

V. PERSONAL FEELINGS

Listening to Our Inner Selves

Living with a Feeling of Frustration

Feelings of Guilt and Insecurity

Accepting Self with a Sense of Humor

Feeling Restless and Seeking Peace

Expressing Love in a Human Way

Signs of Maturity in Religious Life

* * *

Listening to Our Inner Selves

Modern studies in development stress that we should learn to listen to our inner selves. How can we deny self, as the Gospel says, and at the same time listen to self?

* * *

At first sight it may seem as if a serious contradiction exists between listening to self, to my feelings, emotions, and perceptions as recommended by modern studies, and denying self, as Christ invites us to do. (Mark 8:34-38) However, listening to my inner self, to what I feel and desire, is not necessarily contrary to the Gospel dictum to deny self.

Some cultural and religious attitudes of the past may have fostered a negative understanding of self-denial. To deny self meant to ignore my feelings. Feelings were believed to be the "lesser" part of man's nature that "reason" had to control by covering them over and blocking them out.

To deny or repress the signals my feelings send to me would be to cut off part of my God-given nature. My decisions are likely to be wrong if I close myself off entirely from the feeling dimension of self-awareness.

Listening to these feelings does not mean that I will move to satisfy them immediately and directly. Rather I have to dialogue with them.

After a day of intensive study, I might yearn for an evening away from books and papers. My body feels tense and strained. A friend invites me to a play. In deciding whether or not to go, I am influenced by my inner feelings, my strained body, edgy nerves, drained spirit.

Once I become aware of my inner feelings and emotions, they no longer exist like skeletons in the closet, threatening to burst forth when least expected. I am able to direct them in light of my life style and ultimate goals. Out of the different options open to me, I select the one most in accordance with the values that give meaning to my life and the way I have chosen to live them.

I may compare feelings to the shell of a walnut. They are an essential part of me, serving to indicate what I am really experiencing. Feelings are voices that beckon me to listen to what is going on inside me. I listen to what they say but not in isolation from the other dimensions of myself and the reality of my situation. Taking all this information together, I can understand more fully my inner condition.

A doctor who listens to only one symptom in his patient may make a false diagnosis. This is why he listens to many symptoms at once. Similarly I may learn to identify my feelings for what they are and thus avoid making a superficial diagnosis of my behavior.

Being aware of my feelings does not mean acting out of their emotional impact. Neither does it mean repressing or negating them.

Our tendency today may be to think that we must listen to and follow every feeling instinctively and indiscriminately. According to this view, not to live by the movements of the vital me would be to deny that which makes us most human. Freedom of choice is as restricted by idolatry of feelings as by the former attempt to repress them.

As long as the suggestion to be more aware of my feelings does not close me off from the spiritual dimension of life, it can provide valuable insights that help me live my religious commitment more fully. Denial of self may then mean making a decision that places responsibility above desire, concern for others above satisfaction of self.

My response to feelings is not one of negation and repression but of honesty and humility. Often only after I listen can I choose to deny.

Jesus often talked about life in terms of death. And yet He saw no contradiction. About the grain of wheat, He said, we have to let the seed be covered by dirt and decompose. It has to fall apart before a new shaft of wheat will sprout. Death in short precedes true life. (John 12:24)

Look at the changing seasons. Again life out of death. Death—even the death of a treasured idea—can bring new life to the person. In this sense moments of self-denial are life moments, dynamic and immediate. I experience what it means to die in order to be born again. I cease trying to figure out in a purely rational way where inner self begins and outer self leaves off. I come to rest instead within the mystery of paradox that is at the heart of Jesus' message: "Whoever would save his life will lose it, but whoever loses his life for my sake will find it" (Matthew 16:25).

* * *

Living with a Feeling of Frustration

How can a person live with a feeling of frustration without concentrating excessively on it? For example, the frustration that arises in regard to a difficult personal relationship or an assigned task you do not want to do.

* * *

There may be times when a misunderstanding between myself and another extends through the whole day. In the midst of office work or teaching, meals or recreation, something happens that sets off anger, hurt, resentment.

Trying to be nice seems so phony. My efforts at reconciliation are awkward and ill at ease. One part of me wants to accept this person; another part can hardly stand to be around her.

In my frustration, the best I can do for a while may be to avoid her. I stay away, knowing that I will only get upset if I see her. I do not want our difficulties to fill the whole day. I stay away to gain some needed inner calm in order to pray, read, do my work.

Time goes on and I am about to approach this person more directly. One day I invite her to go somewhere with a group of my friends. I surprise myself. I had not consciously thought of doing this. It just seemed natural and right. I realize that at that moment, I feel no animosity. I can extend to her this gesture of friendship and really mean it.

This incident may change my attitude. Afterwards, although my difficulty with her is sometimes magnified out of proportion, it never again has the power to dominate my feelings as excessively as before. There are still times when the best I can do is to withdraw and regain equanimity. There are other times when we talk *at* each other and not *with* each other. But somehow I feel a peace under the pressure. I know that if I keep open to her—talking with her when I can, staying away in order to avoid making things worse—that sooner or later my frustrations with this person will ease up or cease altogether.

This incident shows that a person can live with a feeling of frustration without concentrating excessively on it. In the short run, it may seem impossible; in the long run, it can be done.

I can concentrate in different ways. For instance, I can concentrate on the intricate design of my rug in such a way that everything else in the room becomes a blur. Or I can concentrate on the overall effect of this rug and notice how it blends in with the other colors in the bedspread and curtains.

In both cases the rug is the focus of my attention. In the first instance, however, it absorbs my attention totally; in the second, it is seen as a part related to a much larger whole—my room.

When I find myself frustrated, it may be because I am concentrating on my problems too narrowly. I fail to see beyond them to their relation with the encompassing situation. This is not to say that I should repress my feelings of uneasiness and frustration; on the contrary, I should try to discover what these feelings are telling me about myself.

Noticing how frustrated I become when others do not help with work around the house, I may try to discover why. I realize, after much reflection, that I am projecting my own work demands onto others. When I am not working, I feel guilty. My guilty feelings about not working prevent me from taking the time to relax. This is why the apparent unconcern of others for work frustrates me.

I may have to go through several repeated explorations of this behavioral pattern before my frustration is overcome. This effort takes courage and patience because I find it difficult to be objective about myself. I block out certain truths. Though this "blocking out" is not intentional, it prevents me from understanding why persons who do not work as much as I do frustrate me.

What frustration is saying may not be pleasant to face. It may be tempting to direct my attention outside—to the disagreeable faults in the other or to the imperfections of my current situation—rather than to confront myself with searching questions: What makes this task or person so irritating? Is it because there are things in myself I would rather not know or admit?

What matters is not merely to concentrate on my frustration, but to listen to what it is telling me in the context of my experience as a whole.

I may be able to do little to change the persons with

whom I live or the projects in which I am involved. I can choose, however, what my attitude will be. This choice requires that I make an honest effort to discover what is going on within me that causes this feeling of frustration. Then I can see how this feeling relates to the broader context in which it arises.

Many things occur which I cannot control. I may be struck with a severe illness at the height of a successful career. A loved one may die needlessly. A friend may betray me. A fire or storm may destroy the work of a lifetime. In an instant all my planning is reduced to nothing. I am unable to do anything to reverse the course of events. This example shows how extremely frustrating life can be.

The feeling of frustration, if I live it through well, can be a blessing in disguise. It can teach me at least two lessons, well worth knowing.

The first is about myself and my inability to make this self all I would like it to be. The root of frustration may lie in my desire to control my life according to the plans I decree. This same experience confronts me with the futility and even blasphemy of such a desire.

This realization leads me to a second lesson. From my frustrations, I can learn about the providential will of God and His power and presence in my life. He comes when I least expect Him and His touch is both calming and upsetting. He will ask of me things I had never foreseen or planned on doing. His action in my life may turn me "inside out and upside down," as Chesterton said it did to St. Francis of Assisi.

I cannot learn the second lesson until I have learned the first. Until I have experienced my own limitations, my own inability to save myself, I shall not be able to truly know God as a personal Savior.

Though frustration may at first appear to be a negative

experience, it can be the beginning of deepened insight and further spiritual growth.

* * *

Feelings of Guilt and Insecurity

How can I best handle the feelings of guilt and insecurity that accompany departure from the traditional understanding of a "correct" religious life? How can I be sure that my ideas about the vowed life are not simply manifestations of selfishness or immaturity?

* * *

It is easy to identify correct religious life with faithful and exact fulfillment of detailed prescriptions. This way of living presupposes a real or imagined rule that explicates in detail the way a religious should live in order to remain faithful to her vows.

A person may strive to make this rule her own. She models her life on the "good religious" pattern held up to her over the years. She lives according to the generally accepted norm of doing things. If she acts differently, it may only be because she follows a newer way of doing things correctly.

Whatever the case may be, the center of her life is outside of herself. She is moved to act not from the deepest core of her being but in conformity to an exteriorly established code she has made no effort to personalize.

Perhaps the best way to alleviate guilt feelings that accompany departure from an old and inauthentic way of life is to grapple honestly with the presuppositions that bind me. Guided by the light of Christ, I can search for the central purpose of my life and, against this background, evaluate the "correctness" of any attitude or action I undertake.

As I come to know my center more clearly, I am better able to separate the essential from the peripheral. I find that some of the things for which I feel guilty are really not matters essential to the meaning and living of my religious life but only imagined violations of a rigid, external code of comportment.

Guilt feelings that arise when I deviate from the "correct" way of doing things may also spring from my fear of being different. This guilt of standing away from the crowd is called "separation guilt." It is linked to my fear of being lonely, of feeling cut off from others for not following a traditional or popular style of doing things.

Guilt feelings rooted in separation guilt display certain traits. I become disturbed when others criticize me. I cannot accept their criticism calmly and must either retreat into anonymity or force them to change their opinions to agree with mine. I feel secure only if I am affirmed. I cannot do what I believe in a calm way, witnessing for the values I hold while allowing others to have a view different from my own.

Separation guilt is thus concerned with appearances. I am afraid to be thought of as different by others.

Idealizing guilt is related to separation guilt. I may feel guilty, for example, when I say "no" to someone simply because my refusal does not fit into the ideal picture I have of myself as a thoughtful, responsive, generous person. Guilt from idealizing is most often false because I feel guilty about things that are impossible for me to be or do at this time. When my life becomes an attempt to live up to the "ideal me," I may be driven to act in ways untrue to myself.

Separation guilt thus springs from a distortion of man's yearnings for unity. This unity with God and others is a gift. I cannot force it by fading into the wall of conformity or battering others into conformity with me. Separation guilt signals the failure that necessarily follows any attempt to manufacture unity.

Guilt from idealizing springs from a distortion of man's yearning for transcendence. I distort my innate orientation to Absolute Perfection when I transfer its claim to the visible and temporal. In this world I am always on the way toward becoming my deepest self in the Divine. Never in this life can I attain this self fully.

If I further explore this experience, I may discover that my guilt is due less to a departure from inner life and calling than to the subtle remarks and uplifted eyebrows of others. I may discover that I am more concerned about my failure to live up to my idealized image of a religious rather than my failure to give myself more fully to Christ in prayer.

Keeping up with today's pace may necessitate change and its accompanying insecurity but the abdication of an interior spiritual life cannot take place without arousing feelings of guilt.

* * *

Accepting Self with a Sense of Humor

Can I learn to accept myself, even my "neurotic self," with a sense of humor? I may not feel any better about what I learn but at least I can accept what happens and work from there. Is this the way to listen to God's will on the feeling as well as on the intellectual level?

* * *

It seems as if we live a long time and are well into our commitments before we discover the real gift of our existence. We begin to think things through. We have an insight. This is just the beginning. It takes time to come in touch with all the nooks and crannies of this living me. I have to familiarize myself with all its corners but with care.

Our life is a gift: body, psyche, spirit—all aspects of life are given and all that God has given is good. Our house has many rooms. Each one of us is somewhat unbalanced, onesided, "neurotic", to a greater or lesser degree; but we are much more than that in God's eyes.

Observe a spinning top. At times it seems unbalanced, in danger of toppling over at any second. Then, as it keeps spinning, it brings itself to an upright and balanced position. On the surface what is visible to the observer is an obvious imbalance, while on a deeper level a balanced or centering movement is taking place.

The same thing may be happening in regard to my neurotic anxieties and compulsions. Disintegration occurs to make integration possible. In the midst of chaos, I may become more attuned to my deepest center. My concern shifts from what is limited and temporal to the point where I transcend these limitations and see what new level of centering they are pointing toward.

I am not called by God to be "perfect" in the external sense. I am called to move toward integration on the spiritual level by keeping myself open to the redemptive and purifying action of the Divine. St. Paul said that Christ's power was at its best in weakness. He was happy to make his own weakness manifest so that the power of Christ could live in him. (2 Corinthians 12:9) Can I not do the same in regard to my "neurotic self"?

The irksome nature of my neurotic self may remain with me to my dying day. I may not feel better, if by this I mean not being inconvenienced or embarrassed. I can feel better, however, in the sense of no longer being dominated by the negativity of my neurotic self. This happens when my attitude toward self changes.

An important means of bringing about this change of attitude is staying within the routine demands of daily life. Often we tend to so concentrate on a problem that we begin to isolate ourselves from others. The task to be faced or the problem to be solved grows out of proportion. To avoid this imbalance I need to keep faithful to the performance of daily tasks, to place my own small work and world in the perspective of my life as part of the Christian mystery. Strengthened by the Risen Christ, I realize that even my neurotic self can be a productive agent of growth.

Then I may be able to accept myself and whatever happens to me with that sense of humor characteristic of the saints instead of seeing suffering and failure as an irreconcilable tragedy.

Sense of humor can be seen as a lighthearted understanding and appreciation of who I am before God and man. It allows me to appreciate the fact that I am an odd hybrid indeed; an individual with all sorts of lofty aspirations coupled with quite ordinary and less than ordinary abilities. A sense of humor reminds me of the still odder fact that God allows me to be this way for reasons that presumably seem good to Him through opaque to me on occasion.

God insists on entering into the deepest relationship with me and goes to apparently preposterous extremes—Bethlehem, Calvary—to lure me into this relationship. The absurdity of this intimacy rightly calls for the laughter of faith.

Sense of humor is a prelude to faith. It is a proof of my capacity to gain a vantage point from which to look at myself with all my pretensions, foibles, and conceits.

What is really funny about me is precisely the fact that I take myself so seriously, as if I am the center of the world.

Sense of humor can be a beginning of humility, of accepting myself as I am, in all my ordinariness, with no illusions about myself and no inclinations to appear better than I am, either in the sight of God or of neighbor. Knowing I am loved, accepted, forgiven—belief in the ultimate grounding, meaning, and purpose of my life— are also occasions for joy. This joy expresses itself in that exuberance of which sense of humor is one spontaneous expression.

The freedom to indulge in humor is best expressed in the company of those with whom I have established a relationship of mutual confidence and trust. In this sense, too, humor expresses my intrinsic relation to the Divine. It presupposes a familiarity with God and a union sufficiently established to permit the freedom of light-heartedness and warmth.

Humorous acceptance of self is also a form of courage, the courage to be all that I am, no more and no less. It is self-surrender in a detached sense, a magnificent means of feeling more "at one" with God, of being able to accept myself as He accepts every fiber of my hybrid and often pretentious personality.

Christ did not promise that acceptance of what God allows would necessarily be easy or without pain. He only promised to be with us always, giving us the strength to meet whatever form of suffering God asks us to endure.

* * *

Feeling Restless and Seeking Peace

Is it possible to listen too much? I find myself plagued by a continual sense of restlessness. I see the needs of people and know my efforts to help them are inadequate. I could do so much more. The more I think and listen, the more tormenting is this sense of restlessness. How can I find the peaceful inner feeling I seek, even in the midst of activity?

* * *

When I do not give to others, I feel selfish; if I do not distance myself from others, my life becomes too demanding. There must be a middle way.

I may discover that my restless desire to help is not always motivated by genuine concern. It may stem from some unnoticed or unresolved conflict. It could be that I am acting from a need to be needed. There is a fine line between genuine giving and needy self-fulfillment.

The answer is not to remain immobile until I am sure my motives are pure. I will always act from a mixed bag of motives but my tormenting restlessness tells me to act not quite so frantically or intensely.

Indifference to others does not always signify lack of care. It may mean a healthy forgetfulness that frees me to decide what my stand will be toward personal and interpersonal life experiences.

Some element of restlessness will always remain. It is part of the human condition and apparently will not be stilled until I rest in God. However, a quiet care for self and others, which keeps in mind my human resources and the real demands of the situation, may strengthen the order and harmony of my life. As a happy consequence, I may discover that I am also more effectively able to serve.

There are, of course, hundreds of ways in which I feel inadequate. I could be kinder. I could work harder. I could waste less time. There is no denying this. Nonetheless focusing on where I went wrong in activities and responses may be the cause of my restlessness.

I think too much about what I could have been. I create an "if only" attitude that blinds me to the real possibilities of my life.

To say that I was given that I might give is true; equally true is the fact that I was given for the simple reason that God loves me. He loves me as a person on whom He has lavished His gifts freely and not only as a channel by which these gifts may be passed on to someone else.

The greatest gift I can give to a person is often not what I can *do* for them but what I can *be* for them. If I am restless, I bring them my restlessness. If I am at peace, I bring them my peace.

Daily life is not merely a series of activities that I perform more or less perfectly but an ongoing expression of the Holy Ground and Source of life. In this light I may see my limitations and the needs of the world more clearly. I begin to understand what St. Paul meant when he said, "You know that your toil is not in vain when it is done in the Lord" (I Corinthians 15:58).

For this reason, I need to respect the unfolding mystery of myself in time. I can't do this if I feel I have to keep busy from morning to night. Rushing from task to task, I may miss the precise thing I seek: the person God wants me to be.

If I reflect on my life here and now, I may find that I already possess what I seek, the God-life within me. In the natural and peaceful living of a God-oriented life, I can bless what is mine and thank God for what I can give to others. This quiet living of the inner life lifts me out of the vicious circle of frenzied activity and restless pursuit.

I experience the inner peace of a graced existence rooted in continual response to the will of the Father for me. I seek to maintain a balanced tension between external activity and coming home to my spiritual life by centering in God.

True, I see many needs and I realize that my greatest efforts will always be inadequate to meet them. But my torment and restlessness come not from what I see. They come from my forgetfulness that God sees far more than I ever will in my limited perspective; He alone knows the reason why things are the way they are.

* * *

Expressing Love in a Human Way

Many religious admit they have lost the ability to express their love in a warm human way. Some blame family background, others religious formation. Still others say it is because religious do not experience an exclusive love as in marriage. What are some ways and means of overcoming this seeming lack of love?

* * *

The art of loving is not something I know from the moment of birth but something I must learn as I live and grow.

A small child is not concerned about the welfare of his mother and what he can do to please her for her own sake. He seeks only to fulfill his needs and desires. The child loves his mother, but initially only for what she can give him.

The narcissistic need-love he manifests at this early stage of development is necessary for his survival. He is as yet unable to provide for himself and therefore his major concern must be that another give him what he needs.

As time passes and he is able to do more for himself, he becomes aware that his mother is not merely a provider; she is someone with needs of her own who deserves his love for her own sake. He progresses in this way from an ego-centered to an other-oriented love.

This change of love object from self to others does not exclude my need to still receive the love of others. I both need to love and be loved throughout my life.

If the need to be loved dominates my life, I may lead a totally I-centered existence. In this type of love, I cannot let go of my need for love in order to go out to the other.

If my need to love dominates, I may be totally other-centered, forgetting my own needs in my eagerness to meet his. Other-centered love can be a means of manipulative control. I try to please the other so that he may plea˜ ˜ me.

True love is centered on the other without forgetting my own needs. My movements are in harmony with his because I am first in harmony with myself.

Other-centered love, that emerges out of self-respect, makes me more sensitive to the daily problems of the people around me. I do not consider them mere functionaries. I am open to them as they are in themselves—not simply for what they can do. They in turn are free to love or reject my unique self. My response harmonizes with the personal feeling or need of the other at this moment.

By the same token, the experience of another's love opens me to my ability to love. It helps to form my self-identity, that core of personality that persists throughout my life.

Without some initial experience of being loved, I am likely to keep on expecting others to give me the basis of my identity. Such dependency is precarious, for I tend to take too seriously their disapproval or praise.

Love is not a project to be undertaken in ten easy steps, though it does elicit certain dynamics.

When I am in the presence of someone I love, I try to be fully with him here and now. I pick up his unspoken communications; in my presence he can be his best or worst self without false feelings of guilt, shame, fear, or anxiety.

I do not place unnecessary "shoulds" upon the one I love. These "shoulds" are usually a masked narcissistic demand on my part to look good in social, religious, or familial relations. My love only grows to the degree that I emerge from this narcissism.

Warm human love is expressed through a non-possessive relationship that leaves the other's freedom unhampered and manifests a respect for his and my own moods and modes of behavior.

Should I discover that I lack these expressions of love, I can undertake a disciplined, patient effort to grow in sensitive awareness of the other. But love under no condition can be a willful project. I cannot plan to have soft or sparkling eyes. A warm response just happens. My face softens spontaneously. With eyes and words I address the other from my heart.

Love is thus not something quantitative, the sufficiency of which I can measure. It is a gift and its value lies deeper than any one expression.

A true gift is freely given. I do not give something to someone I love merely from a sense of duty or because it is something he needs. A gift cannot be a means of self-glorification. If my expression of love does not come from within, it will remain artificial.

Love is expressed in our lives not in textbooks or theory but by being true to self and other in situation. It means stopping long enough to see the other as a self, a complex of capabilities, limitations and needs, of noble impulses and mediocrities.

If I want a vivid illustration of what it means to love, I can meditate on the life of Christ. He had about Him an ease, graciousness, and warmth that could draw all hearts. He could touch responsive chords in other human beings. He could share moments of wonder and joy; grief, weariness, or disappointment were not foreign to Him either. He could thrill to the appeal of nature and be delighted by the innocence of a child.

As witnesses for Christ-like love, religious must be careful not to confuse virtuous living with some type of disembodied existence, for human loving will suffer as a consequence. Trying to be other than what we are—flesh and blood human beings—will lead only to the development of a counterfeit love of formal politeness, impersonal tolerance, or vague humanitarianism. We need to return to the truthful reality of our humanness; we are struggling needy persons in a world with others like ourselves, all of us in need of one another and in ever growing need of Christ.

Inspired by His example, our love will be an inspiration to others, enriching us both as givers and receivers of love.

* * *

Signs of Maturity in Religious Life

A person claims to be secure and solid in religious life and yet strikes others as defensive, anxious, and tense. Are such feelings a sign of immaturity and unresolved childhood experience? What are the signs of a truly mature religious dedicated to religious life?

* * *

When there is harmony between me as I am and the world as it is, I am on the road to maturity. I not only know my limitations and talents; I accept them as they are. I accept myself for what and who I am, though I work to correct my faults and failings.

Maturity includes the will to become as fully human and spiritual as possible. If I should fail in my efforts I am not overly discouraged; I continue along the rugged path of personal growth with a perseverance that avoids undue anxiety.

The mature person does not indulge in the "if only" game. Being mature and attaining ever greater maturity means that I not only accept myself as I am; I accept also the limitations and possibilities of the life style I have chosen.

As a religious I know I am no longer open to certain

experiences available to me prior to my consecration. Rather than seeing this limitation as a hindrance to wholeness, I see it as a necessary condition for ordering the world in accordance with my religious hierarchy of values.

Within these limits, I realize, there are infinite possibilities for growth. I accept the privileges and responsibilities proper to religious life and try to meet my commitments with care and sincerity.

My eyes no longer turn toward what I might have been had I followed another course. They are focused on the life I have chosen and the wholeness I may be able to achieve by living it fully.

I realize, moreover, that spiritual and psychological maturity, while not excluding one another, are not the same. I can have all the psychological criteria for maturity and still not be living a spiritual life. How to live the interior life deeply and uniquely is one of the possibilities religious life allows me.

Defensiveness, insecurity, tension, and anxiety may be signs of immaturity and unresolved traumatic experiences, but not necessarily so. Their meaning in terms of health or illness can be best determined by a trained psychologist or psychiatrist.

However, the promise is always there that God's grace can work through such signs of psychological imbalance and be the sustaining means by which the person has the courage to face problems honestly and live with them if they cannot be cured.

Provided the core of my willing life is united to God, even psychological obstacles can be endured if not overcome. No human failing is so great that it ceases to merit redemption.

Having any of the above signs to a degree usually indicates that I am a member of the human race in the process of redemption and growth.

Nature speaks to me of this maturing process in its

ripening and becoming. Stripped of its leaves and fruits by autumn's frost, a tree appears frail and insecure. In the winter it is stark; it moves in the wind with sharp jagged motions, vivid contrast to its gentle swaying in response to a summer breeze or the soft rustle of the wind moving through its leaves in early spring.

Within my life a similar dialogue and response occurs. Alive to the situations in which I find myself, I must vary my manner of being present. Making plans to visit a friend makes me feel joyful. I am excited and happy by the thought of being with her. When my plans are interrupted by a snow storm, I feel disturbed and impatient. I have to rearrange my day in response to this change in nature.

Relationships with other persons display similar dynamics. I may excuse a blunder in one while hesitant to understand the same failing in another. I experience myself reacting to an office crisis impersonally today while yesterday, in an almost identical situation, I was personally concerned.

Everyday living reveals a rhythm in my experiences. The only sameness which seems present is that I find myself in each situation. At times I am tense and insecure. Some may label me immature at such moments. However, I am also aware of a secure and peaceful self-presence in other situations. Aware of the rhythms in my life, I am less ready to categorize myself as mature or immature. Rather than a static typing, maturity implies a dynamic response to life in dialogue with the rhythmical movements of myself and my life situation.

In religious life it is not helpful to present a list of signs by which to recognize when a person is mature. Only when being a religious becomes an irreducible part of my life can I say that I am mature and dedicated. This does not mean that I will cease altogether being defensive, insecure, tense. It does mean I will have a center in which to settle down.

This center is Christ. He is the perfect model of human maturity. His purpose for being among men was that they might have life more abundantly.

Growing in Christ enlarges my capacity for love and service. Secure in the realization that I am valued for what I am, I feel free to be open to others without fear of rejection or hasty labeling. My love can incarnate itself in service to the other according to his individual needs and human resources. Rhythms of loving, giving, and growing are established between us.

As mature and dedicated religious, who are growing in the Christian life, we realize that through Christ we are the possessors of unlimited sources of grace that can foster in us the fullest possible measure of personal growth.

QUESTIONS AND ANSWERS

on

VI. RELIGIOUS LIFE

How Young and Old See Religious Life

Seeking the New and Renovating the Old

Relevance of Religious Life

Necessity for Specialists in Religion

Means of Deepening Religious Life

Living Religious Life on the Level of the Spirit

* * *

How Young and Old See Religious Life

Younger sisters see religious life in an entirely new light. Older sisters differ with them in regard to what a religious is expected to be and do in this post-Vatican age. How can this confusion be resolved?

* * *

A jumbled jigsaw puzzle. That's how religious life seems today. Can this puzzle take on meaning? The pieces of a puzzle fit together when I study each one in its uniqueness and guide it to its own proper place. Ordering these parts takes time and effort, trial and error, perseverance and patience, with an occasional hint from others.

When all of the pieces are properly placed, everyone admires the puzzle; each unique part derives its value from its place in the whole.

The puzzle of religious life is not so much a matter of differences between young and old. The source of confusion is lack of clarity in regard to what the fundamental structures of religious life really are. What belongs and what is superfluous? What is lasting and what is transitory? Attempts to clarify these questions may initially add to the confusion.

Articles may appear by specialists who tend to make central one or the other part of the puzzle to the neglect of the whole. Religious life is identified with work in the inner city or care for the sick.

The secondary aim of religious life (professional service) supercedes the primary aim (the spiritual life and unfolding of each sister.) The primary aim is incarnated in the secondary but the secondary ought never to replace the primary. So-called spokesmen for religious life may disregard its essential tenets or strive to incorporate into this life style practices out of tune with celibate living in community.

Sifting out all that erodes religious life *as religious* is a necessary step in evaluating what changes support and which disregard the total reality of religious life. The appraisal necessary for enlightened renewal requires research into all phases of religious life—old as well as new—a study of the culture in which it appears and of the persons in need of its witness value.

Releasing members from community works for such study takes on new seriousness. Particularly anyone engaged in formation work needs intense preparation. Formation personnel are responsible for the future of religious life, preparing novices to communicate to the culture the essential message of Christ-like living through a consecrated life form.

When I feel the lines of division forming in my community, I want ready answers that will relieve the anger, hurt, and misunderstanding. No such facile replies can be made. Differences of opinion are unavoidable; however, the confusion might be dissolved to a degree if we try to understand why it has arisen. How can we meet and live with it?

The core of religious life expressed in the evangelical counsels has not changed that much since the days of the founders. What has changed is the way in which these counsels are being taught. Older and younger sisters can agree on the need and value of the counsels for religious living. They may differ, however, in their approach to living these counsels. This is not surprising.

Children today live differently from their parents, though still sharing with them certain basic values. We celebrate liturgy with the same reverence for Christ, only the methods and approaches to the Mass have changed. We teach mathematics with the same intensity displayed by a teacher fifteen years ago but our methods have drastically altered. These changes are not the only reality.

Children are still children, meant to be guided and loved on their way to maturity; the liturgy is still the Passion and Resurrection of Christ; mathematics is still the science of numbers. So too in religious life: the vowed life is still a life of poverty, chastity, and obedience.

As our insight into the nature and purpose of religious life develops and matures, it is natural and normal for dissent to occur. Dissent is no reason to split the community into two groups, any more than different methods of child-rearing should split apart parents and grandparents.

If agreement is reached on the essential elements that make religious life religious, then perhaps confusion arises when peripheral values begin to be made central.

In regard to confused areas, each religious needs to remain open to the value concerned. Solutions ought to be based on the criterion of how much they help or hinder the living of the participative religious life as the union of contemplation and action.

Community living may sometimes demand of me the sacrifice of my own suggestions for how to solve our problems. My experience, especially, when I am young, is simply too thin to build a whole community upon. The young may have the zest for change but the old have the wisdom of stability. The two sides need to stand together in order to stem the secular tide threatening the shores of religious and lay life alike.

The bond that unites all members of the community must be their common care and respect for one another as consecrated persons. True concern and respect will transcend differences of approach or opinion. The superior's role must be decisive in questionable matters.

She should use her authority as a means of unifying the different sides.

In a spirit of mutual respect and obedience, communities can open up avenues of communication to air views of the various age groups. Weekly house meetings, workshops, and renewal session are a few possibilities.

As religious are human, so too will confusion and disagreement exist among them; but if they meet these troubled times as mature people of God, they will lead not to disruption but to new growth for both person and community.

Especially is this so in regard to the present emphasis on formation and renewal. Religious want more than ever to focus their attention on the essentials of the vowed life. What gives this life form its identity? For the purpose of renewal some areas may be attended to more explicitly than others. As in any scientific study, one small area, too heavily focused on, may result in a distorted view of the whole. Re-newal, instead of being a balance of the "re" and the "new", becomes a totalizing of one or the other side.

Formation programs especially need to present an integrated view of religious life. The tenets of the vowed life, while basically the same, require certain cultural adaptations. However, the light of this life glows from the same essential core: individual consecration to God in community.

Various phases change and evolve but the basic structures of religious life endure. With this in mind, the study of certain practices of religious living need not cause bitter confusion.

Much of the confusion between young and old is therefore more often a distortion of perception than a real doubt about essentials. The task of formation personnel is to illumine the beauty of living one's whole life in accordance with the will of the Father and with the desire to witness for His way in the world.

Sisters of every age can then see the similarities that bind them as messengers of the Transcendent and be relaxed about the differences changes in externals inevitably evoke.

As long as human beings live together, it is a myth to think that it is possible to remove all causes of division and to live in ideal harmony. Personal experience and history teach us otherwise.

Even the early Christians, who could be identified by their love for one another, were not without serious differences. Tensions can result from background, training, personality clashes, or any number of other sources. To see them disappearing just because of the renewal of religious life is an unreal and unattainable ideal.

Disenchantment and discouragement are bound to result when we compare our actual community with our idealized dream of what community should be. Renewal intends us to become more real. The last thing it wants to do is build false expectations.

Differences and tensions can serve as means to try even harder to establish an atmosphere that sustains each member's personal unfolding in presence to the Holy. Deep respect for and acceptance of each other is essential. In light of our mutual need for redemption, confusion and tension can be seen as steps along the way toward individual and communal development.

If religious life is to be an effective witness for Christ in the culture, it must also adapt itself somewhat to the needs, customs and spirituality of its age.

Due to rapid technological advances, society and culture are changing more in this century than ever before. It is therefore inevitable that religious formed in recent years differ from those who were initiated to ways of praying and acting consonant with an earlier period.

I may find myself clinging to my accustomed way of

living for its own sake rather than making the attempt to update my understanding and living of religious consecration in accordance with post-Vatican directives.

If old and young in religious life are faithful to the vow of respectful openness, their efforts toward renewal will complement one another rather than conflict.

The old may help the young to differentiate the incidental and the fundamental. The young may help the old discover more effective ways to incarnate their deepest religious values in a contemporary society.

Change inevitably involves suffering but to reject needed and wise change is to risk stagnation. All change is an experience of death and rebirth. However, a point of rest and unity can be found among those who differ from one another. It resides in their common search for fitting ways to express the eternal truths they have vowed themselves to witness for.

* * *

Seeking the New and Renovating the Old

It seems as if many young people, seeking religious values, are turning from established centers in order to pursue their goals. In light of this happening, are we to renew the traditional forms of religious life or attempt to found new communities, start all over again or renovate the old?

* * *

You are cleaning a set of silverware treasured by your family. Through use and exposure it tarnishes quickly. An outsider might feel that the time you spend removing the tarnish is wasted. He cannot feel the same way about the silver as you do. He may even advise you to dispose of it and purchase a new stainless steel set. Still you choose to spend the time and energy needed to restore its beauty. The value you experience is in the silver itself, in the family tradition it so beautifully symbolizes.

Polishing removes the surface impurities. The silver remains. Lustre and beauty are restored. Your attempts to renew the silver make its value even more apparent. You know that in time it will tarnish again so to preserve its value you continue to remove the impurities.

The analogy is clear. The aim of renewal is not to throw out the silver of religious life—its essential value—but to clear away the tarnish—the unessentials and mere externals—so that the full value of this life may once again radiate to others.

All living implies a continual need to renew and restore essential values, hidden by various changes but nonetheless present. Through the years, religious life has continued amidst many social and cultural upheavals. Surface tarnishings have accumulated on the traditional forms but the deep value of this life does not change.

Today there is a need to remove the tarnishings resulting from past and present use and misuse. We have to make a choice. Do we believe in the value of religious life? Are we willing to expend the energy essential to restore and renew it? Or do we doubt the value of this life form and feel that it is impossible to revitalize?

In other words, do we polish the silver or throw it away?

Before asking whether successful renovation or building anew is possible, we need to consider a prior question: What really is the purpose of religious life?

So many things have diverted our attention from its essential purpose: the needs of the poor in the inner city, the cry for teachers of catechetics, our own desire for personal freedom, and so on.

We are also heavily influenced by the pragmatic bent of our culture. We want to do something to alleviate these problems. Not a bad intention at all . . . Only the danger is that we may become so preoccupied with what we can do that we forget what we as religious are called to be.

To be centers of religious value radiation and not just service personnel, we need to deepen our spiritual lives first. We need time for quiet prayer and reflection, freedom from preoccupation with monetary or family concerns. In dialogue with past and present masters of spirituality, we need to safeguard the spiritual tradition of Catholic Christian life.

Our struggle to live on the deepest self level will inspire the rest of mankind to live for the highest spiritual values in turn. This witness is the purpose of religious life in the culture. There needs to be some center where these values are kept intact and lived in their fullness or they may be lost to the culture forever.

Religious life is the guardian of religious values. It must preserve them so that men who desire to live these values can find them already lived by religious.

Religious life exists, then, for the personal and spiritual unfolding of its members and the radiation of religious values in the culture. This is also the goal of genuine renewal. Not to throw out the old but to make it speak anew to the present generation whose search for religious values is the same search engaged in by people of the past.

Such renewal may imply leaving already established centers and building anew, but this is more the exception than the rule.

In the beginning, you became a member of your religious community because you wanted to live the highest religious values. You wanted to be true to this unchanging purpose of religious life. Once this purpose becomes clear again, you will want to direct your energies toward its realization. You will want to seriously set about renovating your present centers. How you go about this restoration must always be in dialogue with the original why of religious life.

Many people are seeking religious values but they do not know where to go. Such centers used to be associated with vowed religious living but this association is not so clear any more. Hence the rise and popularity of oriental religions. Witness the widespread use of drugs to induce mystical experiences, the "soul" characteristics of popular poetry and song. All evidence the contemporary search for religious values.

While choosing religious life as a life commitment seems less popular today than in former times, such happenings attest to the fact that religious values are as appealing as ever.

There is a great difference, however, between current methods of seeking the Holy and commitment to the vowed religious life. Practice of oriental religions, smoking pot, listening to soul music demand no final commitment of my life, no integration of these practices into everyday living.

In the vowed life I must be wholly committed. One can stop smoking pot, cease listening to soul music, forego the physical experiences and exercises adapted from oriental religions and be the person he was before he involved himself in these practices. But I cannot forego the disciplines and practices of vowed religious living for any length of time without suffering myself and without affecting others around me.

If I see that essential religious values are absent in my community, I might move to reestablish them by modifying or changing certain structures. The primary criterion for modification and change must be the maintenance of religious values, personally appropriated and lived.

Then, too, there is a great difference between the external manifestation of renewal in constitutions, legislature, and structure, and its inward counterpart: the living of religious values as a follower of Christ.

External structures provide a framework within which I can live my values. As a teacher, I know how vital the environment can be for the developing child. His creativity can be stifled by either excessive rigidity or laxity. His intellectual growth can be thwarted by cultural deprivation.

As a religious, I may rarely experience that sense of wonder so conducive to prayer, if my tight schedule excludes any leisure time. When I am searching for religious values, where do I look? Out there in a rule? Or do I look within?

When I feel the urge to rebel but instead accept the limits of my situation and the persons in authority, I experience what it means to live religious obedience. In this way, obedience is not a rule or an abstract value lived by other people, but a reality in my life. Structures cannot make me obedient if I am not open to this value. I have an obligation to myself, to God, and to my community. It lies in honestly attempting to live the values I profess as a religious.

Another example: I can be told that the practice of silence is essential for prayer and spiritual development but only with gradual growth can I come to a personal awareness of the necessity of silence in my life. No longer is silence simply an ascetic practice or an abstract value; it has become a value for me.

So too with other religious values. As long as I assent to them only intellectually, they are not yet mine. When I have come to an appreciation of values through personal experiences, however costly and painful, they are not readily abandoned. My living deepens and strengthens these values. I make them central in my life and allow them to shape and form my personality.

Environment can facilitate my living of values. A convent atmosphere is generally more conducive to recollection than a college dormitory. Regardless of circumstances, however, I can continue to live my religious values because they are woven into the fabric of my life.

Religious values can be lived within the framework of the religious life style. I know this from experience. Yet religious life today is passing through a phase of purification. Many question and doubt their own relevance and some are leaving.

Are they seeking a new environment for the living of their values? Are they searching for different values to give new direction and meaning to their lives? What does the current turmoil in religious life say to me about my life and values?

What some may forget is that in order to find the Kingdom of God, I must remain in the place where I am. By reexamining my values and the life style in which I have chosen to live them, I may discover that what I am searching for is to be found precisely where I have been all along.

* * *

Relevance of Religious Life

Am I relevant? Coming from religious the question is almost a cliché. Nonetheless the matter still has to be probed. Wherein does religious relevance lie?

* * *

Where can man find ultimate meaning? The separate meanings he discovers in fame or fortune fail to satisfy him. Man always goes beyond the transitory meanings he discovers in search of an ultimate meaning.

This twofold desire of man—his quest for immediate meaning and his urge to find an ultimate center—seems to parallel the dual meaning of the word "relevance."

"Relevance" means to be related to a matter at hand,

and, from the Latin "relevare", it also means to raise or lift up. Meaning is discovered when partial aspects of reality are related in such a way as to form a patterned whole. This relatedness to the whole raises or lifts up each thread of meaning to something that transcends it, namely, to the ultimate meaning of the whole and Holy.

Religious relevance makes it possible for man to take the separate and finite meanings of his life: his joys and sorrows, his successes and failures, his work and play, and relate them to the Sacred or Holy horizon of horizons. In his relationship to God, man participates in a Reality that transcends his own finiteness.

The life of a consecrated religious is a paradigm of the two-fold definition of relevance. A religious witnesses to the meaningfulness of life by relating all finite modes of participation to the eternal and infinite ground out of which every partial activity emerges.

By freeing a religious from family obligations and financial worries, the religious life style provides a structure conducive to recollection and prayer. Because of his freedom to enjoy times of concentrated religious presence, the religious more easily than the average person in the world is able to discern and live a pattern of meaning that demonstrates the eternal dimension of all that he is and does.

The relevance of his life, then, lies in the awareness that he stands among mankind as a living witness to the possibility of finding an ultimate meaning that orders all the finite moments of one's life and raises them beyond themselves to participation in the eternal and infinite.

Many mistakenly equate what is relevant with what is popular. It is not uncommon to read that a particular apostolate is *the* work to do if one wants to be relevant. Today areas of social justice, adult education, and service in the inner city are popular places to be and readily judged relevant.

However, to be relevant implies more than laboring in an area judged relevant by others. Relevancy has to be in tune with my personal unfolding and human potentialities. I have to follow the direction of life that religious consecration and self-awareness point toward. Whether that direction is popular or unpopular by today's standards is of little consequence.

If I allow myself to be seduced by group pressures and judgments, not in harmony with my deepest aspirations and strivings, I may neglect the development of my own graced potentialities.

What if Einstein, in order to be relevant, had taken on the cause of social justice or if Martin Luther King had become a research scholar. The choice would have been unfortunate for each of them as well as for the culture as a whole.

Their unfolding in light of their unique calling provides an excellent example to each of us to respond to our deepest values in a personally relevant way—whether others think our choice is relevant or not.

To ask where relevance lies calls for a response to weave our personal unfolding into the fabric of culture, whether we become nurses, cooks, scholars, artists, or social workers. In each situation, true relevancy lies in the juncture of my calling and the culture's needs.

Two kinds of relevance are exemplified by the relevance of a bestseller and the relevance of a literary classic.

The bestseller is read, understood, and enjoyed by many. It addresses itself to issues, situations, and feelings the majority of people easily recognize. Its language and message are sufficiently uncomplicated to be grasped by the masses. However, bestsellers, with few exceptions, are ephemeral works. They seldom outlive their century or even their decade. The typical bestseller is concerned with temporal and local questions; hence, response is temporal and local. Its relevance is passing. It blazes brightly for a short while but soon burns out.

The literary classic, on the other hand, may go unrecognized in its own time or gain only limited popularity. It continues to be reread and reproduced from age to age. It represents a response to the deeper dimension of what it means to be human. Rooted in time, it nevertheless transcends time and articulates those realms of human life that are ever present and mysterious. Because King Lear touches the eternal questions put forth by its characters, it promises to touch the eternal in its readers.

Like the relevance of a literary classic, the relevance of religious life lies in its capacity to awaken in man his presence to the Eternal. As a consecrated religious, I live my life in such a way that my many acts of temporal service to man, world, and self are centered in the Eternal. I see, as it were, through and beyond the passing issues of the local culture in which I am inserted to its fundamental ground.

Many may not be able to grasp the relevance of the consecrated life because they have lost touch with the eternal roots within themselves. But I should not barter my vision of truth for any degree of popular acceptance or the fleeting reward of momentary relevance.

Neither should I remain callous to the immediate issues of my time. However my life is a call to look steadily at the immediate until my gaze can pierce through its changing tumultuous surface and rest in the still depth of transcendence.

Like Christ, who was extremely irrelevant by the standards of his day, I must listen first to the will of the Father speaking in the deepest recesses of my heart and out of this listening hear the real cry of a people for its God.

My participation in the culture can only be religious to the degree that it flows from my presence to the Holy. I respond in a certain way because I am a religious. The attitude not the action is what counts. I can be religious while typing a letter as well as while praying in the chapel. The religious realm of the action comes not from the action itself but from the way I perform that action.

There is a tendency today to identify activity or involvement with religious relevance. A person deeply involved in the healing of social ills may be religious but he is not necessarily religious because he is involved. Prayer and contemplation are the primary ways by which a religious receives the strength of mind and peace of soul he needs to become actively, not overly, involved.

I must also distance myself occasionally from my task to see if this is what I should be doing for the Lord. Are my talents properly focused so that my presence to God is increased rather than decreased?

If my inner attitude of presence is unduly disturbed, am I taking steps to restore this sense of peace? I should be conscious at all times of what contributes to and what counters my life of prayerful listening to the Lord.

Where does religious relevance lie? The Christian response is everywhere. Man works toward the uplifting of all creation so that all men may raise their hearts and minds to the Lord.

In every age men and women in both single and married life by living religiously demonstrate in ordinary events and situations the art of living in true presence to the Eternal order of reality. Likewise in every age some of these men and women have chosen to consecrate their lives in a special way by witnessing to the relevance of religion.

Their respect for historical events, for others, for material goods is demonstrated by the threefold path of obedience, celibacy, and poverty. By living these attitudes they hope to lead others to the art of raising in worship all situations, persons, and things.

Inherent in their total consecration is a profound sense of wonder that God should endow man with the capacity to participate in drawing all things to Him. No one thing is too insignificant to arouse reverence. Wherever a man worships, there one finds religious relevance and religious experience.

The functional mentality of the present often stifles the fundamental sense of wonder so spontaneous in primitive man. Rather than experiencing awe in the face of mystery, modern man concentrates on probing for solutions. He does not spare the time necessary to recenter himself in the transcendent dimension of reality.

This merely functional approach may affect those who have consecrated themselves to Christ in religious life, so preoccupied are they with discovering where, when, and how man can best be present to the Lord. So pervasive is their anxiety to find answers that they often miss the invitations to wonder and worship that wait all around them.

Those for whom religion is an ever-deepening awareness of the loving Spirit sustaining each person, thing, and event encountered testify to the fact that at all times and in every place man uplifts the culture by acknowledging its ultimate dependence on the Divine.

* * *

Necessity for Specialists in Religion

If the Spirit breathes where He will, why is it necessary to have specialists in religion?

* * *

Ours is a world of specialization. Specialization always demands structuring to be effective. Not so a hundred or so years ago. Seldom was there need to acquire goods outside the home. Most families were agricultural. Their pace was slower. Closeness to nature made their bond with the Creator a pervading part of everyday life. Yet even then there were men and women who embraced religion as a form of life to deepen for themselves and the culture the spiritual dimension of existence.

Nowadays, however, the family is no longer the center for the production of life's necessary goods. Fewer people live close to nature. The natural rhythms of life—planting, growing, and harvesting—are quite unknown to them. Their dependence on the Creator and His presence to them becomes less evident in the bustling cities and super-markets that sprawl across our country. For many, life becomes identified with superficial values and pleasures.

Some people can remain in our society and withstand these attractions. Despite the hectic pace of life, they continue to center themselves in what is essential: their orientation to God and His manifestation in all of reality.

Yet many more people are unable to do so. They succumb to the pressures and pleasures of the technological world. For the sake of these people and the culture as a whole, it is desirable that some persons adopt the religious life style with whatever structures this specialization might entail. Though being a specialist in spirituality is my life call, I may still ask myself at times if I could not live this specialty more intensely outside the structure of my present religious community. It helps to weigh the alternatives open to me in two concrete life situations.

My married brothers and sisters are religious people, but because of the overwhelming responsibility of a family, financial burdens, social pressures, and emotional ties, they are less likely to relate their immediate involvements to the Sacred as easily as I may do.

Likewise, the demands made on my unmarried brothers and sisters by the social system in which we live curtail their freedom for fostering presence to God. Necessarily their time and attention is given to attaining immediate values and goals, through ultimately they may relate these to an eternal goal.

If I really understand what it means to be a specialist in spirituality, I can appreciate anew the freeing structures of my religious community.

A specialist in any field needs an atmosphere conducive to the progress and growth of his specialty. The research scientist needs a well equipped lab, the quiet necessary for experimentation, the availability of scientific literature, the support and collaboration of other research scientists.

The specialist in spirituality needs an atmosphere in which he can have time for experiencing more intense moments of prayer. These times are not a luxury for a specialist in religious presence; they are a necessity, especially for the active religious who is always in danger of becoming entrapped by the demands of his profession.

The structures of my religious community free me from the tyranny of a legalistic corporation mentality, where production and consumption are the primary values. The support and inspiration I receive from the members of my community help me to lead a serene and joyful life capable of inspiring my fellow man to make God the center of his life too.

Over the centuries certain practices that facilitate interpersonal living as well as an increase of man's presence to God are passed down in oral and written form. Specialists are necessary if the values of a fundamental life form are to be preserved. Since values are only revealed in living, a life form rather than an avocation is essential.

Religious men and women replace the structures of the married and single states with those that primarily facilitate religious openness. No structure totally suits every member of a group. Living and appropriating the structures, however, frees one to become increasingly open to the Sacred as revealed in self, others, and world.

Just as there are philosophical centers offering the opportunity for intellectual exchange and communities of artists in which the aesthetic dimension of man is safeguarded and deepened, so too there are communities of men and women who group themselves to live, in whatever darkness, the religious dimension of existence. Their effort is human, their failings many, yet their contribution significant.

Each of us is to be a specialist in religion in the sense that each is to be present to the Holy in the unique way in which his life unfolds.

The parent is called to such presence in the family; the religious in his community. And today, to the degree that religious values are lost sight of in the culture, the religious community of specialists is even more necessary.

History reiterates that the religious life form will last as long as people choose such a way because the Lord has chosen them. The current questioning of its existence and necessity may well be an expression of healthy dissatisfaction and a call to renew my own spiritual life.

* * *

Means of Deepening Religious Life

In searching for means of deepening our religious lives, a merely academic approach will not suffice. However, what if we fall into the other extreme of anti-intellectualism? Will we be able to make decisions that will be universal enough and well thought out enough to last?

* * *

The history of religious life is both cyclical and spiral. That is, repetitive events are balanced by progress and evolution. In the past, great emphasis was placed on a spirituality that looked somewhat askance at education because of the potential danger of intellectual pride. With time, however, the pendulum swung to the opposite extreme. Education was hailed as the only hope for religious if they wished to be effective in the world.

At present we witness a growing desire to return to a spirituality that tends to be less academically based and more in tune with life. Fortunately, the pendulum has not completely swung to the extreme of condemning education as harmful. Religious today have the challenging opportunity to contribute to the spiral movement of history by demonstrating the feasibility of living a balanced spiritual life.

The recent past has taught us that academic formation alone is insufficient. Likewise experience points out the tragic error of exalting intellectual ability and emphasizing it to the exclusion of the emotional and spiritual dynamics that make up the composite structure of man. By the same token, to blindly exclude intellectual pursuits is to deny one of God's gifts to man.

For a balanced approach to the spiritual life two extremes must be avoided: the intellectual view that militates against traditional spirituality, merely because it is traditional, and urges that past structures be thoughtlessly discarded; and the anti-intellectual stance that fiercely maintains the glories of the past, merely because it is the past, and seeks to preserve the status quo. Neither approach will solve the difficulties of religious living today.

An analogy may clarify this point. When an intricate tapestry is viewed two human capacities make the experience pleasing and profitable: one is the ability to analyze; the other is the ability to synthesize.

The former draws attention to the details of the pattern; the latter integrates the beauty of each part into an integral perception of the work of art as a whole.

The first approach is more intellectual in nature. The second involves a more total personal response and usually leads to a judgment. For appraisal to be truly accurate, the analytic and the synthetic functions must be integrated.

The same may be said of decisions about spiritual living. There must be study and dialogue; but these will be ineffective without periodic distancing in recollection and prayer. The fruits of mental activity must be integrated with the initiation into religious and spiritual life.

A balance between the speculative and the practical, the intellectual and the less intellectual, will aid religious in a renewal that contributes to the cyclical and spiral unfolding of religious life.

Religious communities have to combine the theoretical and the practical approach in order to make decisions that will benefit present and future members. Certain members of a community have to concentrate on both intellectual and practical areas in accordance with personal taste and talents.

In our society, as we know, people are forced to specialize. By so doing, they gain insight into a select dimension of reality. If religious communities are to survive, they must see to it that some of their members specialize in research concerned specifically with the religious life form in its spiritual and professional needs.

When these specialists collaborate and communicate with one another, an integrated approach to community living may emerge.

Any mature person recognizes the onesidedness of his approach to reality; he feels the need to be open to the insights of other specialists. This awareness leads him to appreciate the contributions of others. He can then more readily put up with the difficulties involved in making sound decisions of lasting value. By practicing patience, he acquires the ability to give and take and is more willing to give up preconceived and biased ways of reforming religious life.

In our openness to one another, we become open to the Spirit, receive new life, and make room for further growth.

Whether the emphasis is on activity or passivity, academics or anti-intellectualism, immersion or distance, we tend to find ourselves in an either/or mode of life—at times contrary to our best will to be otherwise.

We may live each day in a fragile though living faith, aware that a way of life is not just one decision of universal magnitude or a combination of pat solutions to pat situations but a daily living and uncovering of our deepest potentialities. To live on this level necessitates communion with God, self, others, and world.

The underlying permanent values of religious life are always distinguishable from their concrete particular manifestations. We must discover the core of religious life and then, living at that core, immerse ourselves totally in daily living with its routines and unexpected revelations.

Approaching my life and circumstances from this perspective, I see that the decisions I or my community make with regard to our day to day life cannot totally sustain future generations. However, those made with regard to the permanent values of religious living will reflect a much greater universality.

Meeting my life situation is often a matter of meeting the needs of the moment—for instance, inner city work, CCD teaching, ecumenical dialogue. So my decision to participate in these concrete tasks is likely to be only temporary. It is a different matter, however, when I consider those permanent values of religious living that must be brought to my concrete participation.

It would be untrue both to my religious and professional commitment if, in light of work in the inner city, I were to decide that the best way of serving the population would be to neglect prayer and disregard all the essential safeguards of celibacy.

A decision like this cannot be lasting, for it is contrary to the basic core of religious life. Before long both I myself and those who rely on me, will perceive this discrepancy. Either I have to return to a more faithful expression of religious values or risk having to leave this life form entirely.

When I am imbued with the values of religious living, decisions affecting my life will be illumined by these fundamental values. Prayer and celibacy will always be preserved. I will maintain a healthy balance between the practical and the intellectual. I can immerse myself fully in my immediate situation and yet remain present to the ultimate meaning it reveals.

* * *

Living Religious Life on the Level of the Spirit

I entered religious life and went through my novitiate keeping the rules and doing little else, and now, after many years, I feel bored and empty. How can a person like me begin to live on the level of the spirit?

* * *

Each morning a little old man walks slowly down the road to the river. He listens to the birds singing and calling to each other, watches the water flow down stream, and notices the branches—caught, freed, and moved along by the current. Occasionally children gather around him on the grass. He tells them stories which capture their interest and stimulate their imaginations. His words do not come from preconceived plans. Rich and memoral experiences well up that reflect his simple and wholehearted living of the given moment.

By contrast the project-centered orientation of our technical society predisposes us to see all of life in terms of plans and techniques. The old man shows us, however, that following a plan is not the only path to contemplation and may even be a hindrance.

The life of the spirit is not automatically attained by following certain steps.

As the old man sat on the river bank, he was aware of immediate reality and of something deeper. He spent time there. Patient, unhurried, relaxed, he returned again and again to the riverside. He saw what was there and allowed it to be. He could appreciate the river's ceaseless life and marvel at its ever changing face.

The life of the spirit is not a project to be completed. Neither is it so that one simply sits back and expects it to happen. Being open to the Sacred does not mean living in a vacuum. I have to cultivate a way of living that promotes openness to the Divine.

In this recollected mood, I begin to recognize some of the obstacles that block my presence to God: my overly functional approach to life, a tendency to dominate and control persons and events, a failure to take time for leisure, a tendency to give up in the face of dryness and the apparent futility of my prayer.

The life of the spirit is a rhythm of waiting, gradual change, and dying to self in order to be reborn on a deeper level of life.

I might like it when another person is willing to lay aside her ideas for the sake of someone else's. When I have to give up my ideas, however, the story is different. Similarly the life of a person living on the level of the spirit seems so attractive, but when I attempt to live likewise my actions may seem meaningless.

When I admire the spiritual lives of others and ask how I can live like them, I may be tempted to concentrate on what I can do rather than on who I can be. I might adopt the outward behavior of someone I admire, a move that inevitably leads to discontentment. What is more tragic, I may be so taken up with external appearances that I fail to develop my own unique self.

To open myself to this deeper dimension of the life of prayer, I need to become increasingly aware of who I am in light of my concrete life task. The more I awaken to the spirit within, the more readily will this spirit overflow into every facet of my daily life. I become more sensitive to the changing needs of my situation, less rigid in my responses.

Perhaps the greatest danger I face in searching for a way to deepen my spiritual life is spending too much of my time looking outside of myself.

When I find myself in a depressive mood, wondering if my life has really been worthwhile, I may find myself filled with emptiness and resentment. In certain instances I may come close to despair. But from this depth, I can rise to a greater level of understanding. Pain often precipitates a reflective attitude on my part. I begin to seriously face some fundamental questions: Where am I going? How am I getting there? Can life have greater meaning for me?

I find that meaning is woven out of past, present, and future. In my past I have to accept the negative as well as the positive aspects of my history. Confronted with the present, empty and boring as it is, I realize the need to rediscover selfhood within my lived situation. The future lies before me, a time in which I can shape creatively what I have begun to see.

Throughout this reflection I sense the redeeming power of Christ's love, forgiving me for the past, comforting me in the present, promising his fidelity in the future. I seek now that serenity of God in which I am most deeply rooted.

With eyes of faith, I see the will of God unfolding in my life in a mysterious way, even if I cannot account rationally for every event.

My changed attitude is echoed by Dag Hammarskjold:
"For all that has been—thanks!
To all that shall be—yes!"

Neither my emotions nor my practical ability to organize my life are in opposition to the life of the spirit. The challenges of daily living require efficient task-oriented behavior supported by a strong body and a well balanced emotional life.

In and through my vital and practical life, I hear the invitation to live on a still deeper level of self, that of spirit. On the self or spirit level, I experience inner freedom. I continue to be faithful to the rules and responsibilities of daily life but my inspiration for living emerges from my presence to the Holy Spirit.

What was once felt as a negative experience, boredom and emptiness, may come to be viewed as an invitation to deepen my spiritual life. The call to live on the level of the spirit may come to me during the most boring and arid moments of life. For days I may stare out of my window at a drab parking lot while a lush garden is just around the corner.

Or else I may brood in loneliness while down the hall a person longs for someone to talk to.

In both instances, life seems to escape me. Yet to enjoy the garden or to converse with the other, I must realize they are there. As long as I am unaware of what is given, I may miss out on a chance to live a richer spiritual life.

For part of this givenness is spirit. My spirit puts me in touch with life. It can make the boring and empty, alive and meaningful. It can inspire me to make sense out of apparent nonsense.

I may try to awaken my spirit by the diversion of travel or

escape from the functional world into the seeming blissful universe of drugs, but my life cannot be devoted to these kinds of trips. For the most part it is quite ordinary. The question is, how do I inspirit this ordinariness?

Are paltry things like cleaning my room or preparing my class worthy of such inspiriting? Shouldn't I live these actions through without a second thought? By no means. For spiritual life is about that second thought, that respectful look which sees the same old thing in a brand new way.

There is worth and beauty in the desk top I am dusting, in the lesson on fractions I repeat, in the last hectic moments of class dismissal, in the dainty handkerchief I am about to iron.

To experience this beauty, to be in tune with it, I must be able to look again. From time to time I need to step back and step aside.

By this inward movement, I distance myself from the immediate impact of working, eating, doing, from my public life of sociability and communication. I am able to look again at all these activities, to find their deeper ground. I try to discover who I really am and this discovery helps to unveil the truth of all that is.

One practical means of fostering an interior life is the keeping of a daily journal. Here, while recalling the ordinary events of life, I become present to them in an insightful way. I come to know my patterns of response, my motivations, needs and drives. I learn to recognize selfish mannerisms as well as to appreciate the finer qualities of my personality.

My natural interiority is illumined more and more by grace. If I am receptive to the gift of grace my faith grows into a lived faith. God becomes a Person, real for me. I am able to unite my will to His. I may feel as if my life is just beginning, though chronologically it may be half way over.

I need not be discouraged, however, for even St. Teresa of Avila, in her later years, often prayed, "Lord, teach me to be a good beginner."

Thus the failures, limitations, and weaknesses of my past, which can be a hinderance to the life of the spirit, can also be a preparation for this life if I come to a renewed remembrance of the redemption and if I do not sit in self judgment.

It was while Saul was living out his zeal as a Pharisee that he met Christ on the road to Damascus and, as Paul, came to the realization of the "freedom of the Sons of God."

In the same way, there is nothing in my past that cannot be sanctified through the power of the Holy Spirit, provided I take up my life as it is in a spirit of gratitude. For all the people and events that God has allowed into my life have made me the unique openness to the Spirit I am now.

QUESTIONS AND ANSWERS

on

VII. RELIGIOUS FORMATION

Novices and the Canonical Year

Relation between Formation and Crisis in Religious Life

Formation Centered on the Spiritual

Encountering the Essential in Religious Life

Necessity of Structure in the Novitiate

* * *

Novices and the Canonical Year

In our present talk of renewal, some have proposed that during the canonical year novices should be more available for apostolic work, visiting the sick and poor, teaching catechetics. In other words, they say, complete withdrawal is no longer psychologically sound.

* * *

Even in the most solitary of confinements, we never withdraw completely, for we always bring with us the richness of our past experiences and our future hopes. Nonetheless, to speak of complete withdrawal during the canonical year frequently conjures up thoughts of boredom and restlessness, the seclusion of sprawling farmlands.

Influenced by certain psychological theories which onesidedly focus on the necessity of encounter, some communities have begun to bring novitiates closer to the cities. Some even allow the canonical year to take place in the actual climate of the apostolate.

Whenever we withdraw we do so for a reason. We withdraw from those things that hinder our purpose. During the honeymoon, for example, the newlyweds do not withdraw from circumstances that will help them to know one another. They only leave behind the work-a-day world that may hinder their initial intimate encounter. Similarly, those who enter religious life do not withdraw from everything, only from those things that may hinder the uncovering of their deeper and more fundamental openness to God.

The temporary withdrawal of the novitiate is meant to be an "informed" distancing under the direction of a spiritual master who can aid the novice in the personal unfolding of her unique personality while growing more intimate with God.

During that year, some dimensions of meaning have to be accented while others temporarily recede. This informed withdrawal also allows for a transformation of awareness, a reestablishment of priorities, and a deepening of the call to religious life already heard by the novice.

This withdrawal should help to free the initiate from at least a few of the hindrances that keep him from deepening his primary openness to God. It is a period prayerfully in tune with those values dearest to him as a person.

Not only is such an informed "complete" withdrawal psychologically sound; it is a human necessity. If this precious time of transformation is filled with activity, it may confuse rather than accent the fundamental effort of the novitiate year.

Of what use, some will ask, is a year spent primarily in reflection and prayer? There are problems in the world that cry for solution. Young people are eager to work for such solutions. Why keep them so confined?

Another argument goes this way: if novices are preparing for a profession in an active religious community, why not gear their novitiate toward involvement in the apostolate? Without this active involvement their profession will be divorced from reality.

The thinking behind these questions sounds convincing, but is it? When we look closely at the nature of the human person and the meaning of religious living, we see the need during novitiate to distance oneself from constant involvement in the problems of the world outside the novitiate. Why is this so?

It is not alien to the purpose of the novitiate that novices may have an occasional and limited involvement in the apostolate. However, such involvement can take away from the primary purpose of the novitiate: to set the person on the road to living spiritually. Later in the juniorate comes the question of how to integrate prayer and participation, recollection and action.

There are times in life when all men face major decisions that will affect and determine their entire lives. Undoubtedly the greatest of these concern the choice of a style of life.

When a young man finds a partner with whom he hopes to share his life, he will often distance himself for a while from the one he has chosen. He does this to know her better as well as to decide if married life is the right style of life for him to undertake.

The same principle applies to the person who has chosen the religious style of life. In order to come to a better appreciation of the meaning and demands of this life, the novice distances himself from direct involvement in other possible forms of life and other activities. By freeing himself temporarily from the captivating preoccupations of the world around him, he tries to discover, under the guidance of his spiritual master, if his desire to give himself wholly to God as a religious is genuine or not.

To attempt to force this discovery or to obstruct it by adding countless outside activities is to do him an injustice. He needs time and silence for this discovery. To deny him this time is to risk a future of religious living and activity that may prove to be at odds with one another.

Through occasional activities chosen for their formative qualities, the initiate will not be removed from reality but will be learning to deal with it in its deepest dimensions. Unless he experiences this transcendent horizon, his coming to religious life may turn out to be as fruitless for him as for the culture he wants to serve.

"Withdrawal from reality," is, of course, never

psychologically sound. The person who runs from uncomfortable situations avoids honest confrontation with the world. But is this the essence of the canonical year? To escape the world? To avoid its reality? Is its purpose to create some garden of paradise where young men or women can live unsullied by reality?

If such withdrawal were to characterize the canonical year, it would be psychologically unsound. But novitiate withdrawal means something else.

When a person is judged ready to enter novitiate, his intention is to develop the religious dimension of his being to a special degree. He feels a need to withdraw from activity in order to live with others who are living a like call. Living in a mode of receptivity prepares him to stand in presence to the Holy.

Upon entrance to the novitiate, the young candidate may welcome a time of withdrawal in order to develop his personal relation to the Lord, self, and others.

We could liken this growing relation to God to the relation of friendship. To grow, friendship requires time, discussion, sacrifice, and care. True friendship presupposes that the persons involved maintain their own personal identity and integrity. Often it is necessary for the friends to withdraw from one another in order to find their identity and avoid a manipulative or seductive relationship.

Just as the unfolding of friendship is dependent on the growth of each friend's personhood, so my relation with God keeps pace with my personal unfolding.

I need to take the time to be present to Him in prayer. This will not happen unless I withdraw temporarily from my work and direct myself in a special way to God.

The religious novitiate affords such a time and place of withdrawal. Here the young person can discover his spiritual identity and learn to preserve it amidst his interpersonal relations.

Spiritual identity and interpersonal relations are basic for one who intends to do apostolic work. More importantly, they are essential for a sound relationship with God. The main aim of the novitiate is to build my personal relation to God so I can return to activity without losing sight of the Source of my life and the lives of those I will serve. In light of this purpose, withdrawal is both growth producing and psychologically sound.

Why do problems arise from the traditional withdrawal from secular studies and apostolic activities in the canonical year of the novitiate?

Two main causes may be cited: First, because of premature entrance into the postulancy, the novice may find herself confronted by the canonical year before she is psychologically ready for the experience of laying the foundations of a deep spirituality. This complex process presupposes that the young person has passed through the earlier stages of adolescence and has already begun to discover herself as a unique individual with a personal call to live in presence to the Lord in a special way.

Secondly, because of the decline of real spirituality in the West, and the substitution of behavioristic and intellectual training, the novice might be tempted to weigh spirituality by productive activities that show concrete results. Whereas real spiritual formation is challenging and absorbing, behavioristic or pietistic training may soon become routine and boring. "Let's move the novice out to the missions," may then become the rallying cry of the community.

The novice may look longingly at the apparently exciting and relevant works other sisters are doing. By contrast withdrawal looks so drab and useless. Moreover, the self-confrontation and psychological crisis that must occur from time to time if spiritual transformation is to take place, can be frightening.

The novice seeks a world in which she imagines herself

leading a successful fight for civil rights or counseling troubled teenagers. She may cherish the illusion that she is capable of confronting the complexity of human misery without having first confronted the pre-conscious motives and needs that may have prompted her in the first place to escape the prosaic realities of herself, her fellow novices, and her directress.

There are many kinds of withdrawal. One kind, not so readily recognized, is withdrawal from the painful reality closest to oneself in favor of becoming lost in a round of activities where one can avoid confronting the uncomfortable and puzzling questions: Who am I? Why am I here? What really motivates me? Yet these are the questions no novice can avoid without betraying herself and her life call.

Not all people have the opportunity to take one year off from the busy to and fro of daily living to devote themselves exclusively to personal and spiritual growth. Religious have this privilege. Called to witness for the eternal horizon behind every cultural appearance, they need at least one year to begin the search for the Sacred in themselves.

In our haste to increase what is effective and dispense with what appears detrimental, we often fail to consider the basic ground of religious structures.

In no area of human concern and productivity is there a visible growth without a previous period of invisible deepening.

Engineers delve far into the earth before they begin constructing a building that will be able to withstand the elements. The farmer plants his seed long before he looks for the fruits of his labor. The loving mother speaks to her baby with no expectation of a reply.

So, too, visible growth or unfolding before God requires a period of interior development. Because of the rapid pace of living in our culture, it is extremely difficult for a young person to discover herself and establish a relationship with Christ while in the midst of apostolic labors. Necessary and praiseworthy as these may be, she needs a chance for active withdrawal and communicating in silence.

The purpose of the canonical year was never intended to be one of coffin-like seclusion. Withdrawal was a movement away from overinvolvement in the pursuit of power, pleasure, and possession as ultimates, in order to become respectfully present to self, others, events, and things as manifestations of the Sacred.

Withdrawal is not only a holding back from; it is a holding back for. The canonical year is a preparation for life consecration. A novice during this time stands back from certain activities in order to find herself. Only then is she free to vow her life in poverty, celibacy, and obedience.

Having responded to her life call, at its Source, she is ready to participate more actively in the culture. Moreover, she is sensitive to her need to periodically withdraw to recollect herself and her activities in God. If she never has the opportunity early in life to distance herself from overinvolvement, she may not be aware later of seductive attempts to alter the priority of her values.

This year of silence, recollection, and self-discovery, far from being a denial of what is best for human growth, ought to be considered the most vital period in the formation of the person as religious. Future growth and unfolding are dependent on the novices' capacity to discover the presence to God that she already is. The more active her later life may be, the more necessary this year of formation becomes. Unless the young religious falls back and reflects on the ground of her being, she too may remain alone, like a seed without soil, sterile in her relationship to Christ and unfruitful in her labor for His people.

* * *

Relation between Formation and Crisis in Religious Life

Many of us in our late 30's or early 40's missed a deep period of initiation and formation in the life of the spirit. Now we are faced with the current crisis in religious life as well as with great changes in our respective communities. As a result many in our age group are leaving religious life. How can we face this crisis and overcome it from within?

* * *

While it is true that deep initiation in our formative years may have served to lessen somewhat the present crisis we are in, it would not have removed it. Each of us experiences his own personal crisis at each stage of growth: fetus, infant, adolescent, adult. The variables are different, depending on our personal history and self-concept, on the distinctive way we meet change in any form.

Social upheaval and consequent loss or change of values increase the intensity of the crisis. Our own ground seems to be giving way. Even the supportive ground of church and society does not seem as stable as it used to be. Much that was valued by previous generations is up for grabs today.

It is at this moment of crisis that we are asked to make our values known. Have we interiorized them or not? Each new crisis can be an occasion for reaffirming our lives and our values. The self-awareness gained as a result of crisis forces us, moreover, to search for the ground of our values, to rededicate ourselves to living Christian religious life in a time of transition.

I can be aware of the relation between myself and the world in simple ways like recognizing the effect variations in nature have on me. A cold, bleak November day mirrors my bleak and somber mood. A crisp day in January gives me a positive feeling of life. By experiencing these changes of mood, I can come to a better understanding of the way more major changes affect my life.

Experiences of crisis and confusion offer me a choice: I can be overcome by them or I can become through them.

Despair, confusion, and fragmentation in myself and my community have a definite affect on me. Instead of first seeking the cause outside of myself, I might ask if there could not be a crisis occurring within me. Possibly a natural crisis was pending for me anyway about this time, regardless of the changes occurring in religious life.

Physically, I am becoming more aware of my limits; I tire more quickly; routine more easily becomes a burden. In the social context of community, I am moving into an older age group. Looking back I may wonder if the past years have been fruitful. I try to envision the future, speculating on what I can do to overcome my sense of boredom and frustration.

Throughout this "crisis of the limits," I may forget the present moment and turn instead to prophets of doom who predict that the phasing out of religious life has begun. They claim that it is not "relevant" in today's world. Such opinions likewise make me feel confused and insecure. I may even find myself at times despairing.

Yet where there is feeling there is life. My experience is not one-dimensional. I find that I am also in the world as hoping. In this mood of hope, I see the crisis in religious life as a time of purification. The turmoil within me and the crisis without, whether in community, church or society, become opportunities to experience myself in the here and now.

Changes in community bring me to an awareness of changes in myself. The cause of my confusion is not just outside of me but in me as well.

When Christ invited Peter to walk to Him on the water, Peter strode firmly ahead so long as his attention was on the Lord. When he began concentrating on himself and the nature of what he was doing, he began to founder and sink. With eyes turned again toward Christ, his equilibrium was restored. (Matthew 8:23-27)

Religious today are walking on troubled waters. In many walks of life, escapism seems the favored technique for avoiding the frustration and tension that inevitably arise in human and social life. The premium on fidelity and perseverance gets smaller and smaller. Shallowness and superficiality abound.

Troubled times breed either the most stalwart of souls or spawn the most cringing of cowards. Yet the person who has a Why in his life can put up with almost any How. This thought of Viktor Frankl's might well be a saving one for religious today. It is also a daring challenge.

I have to reexamine the Why of my commitment, purify my motivation, deepen my centeredness in Christ, and strengthen my fidelity to my commitment. Then the various hows that constitute the externals of religious living and cultural participation will flow from my personal life of worship and witness for Christ.

The crisis in religious life today can thus be the occasion for a deepening of faith in Christ. Faith dispels crippling fear and disillusioned apathy. Personal honesty in regard to myself and the living of my commitment helps to keep me faithful.

Christian optimism and joy sustain me in times of anxiety and turmoil. Regardless of my period of formation, this joy is a telling feature of the religious person's vibrant heritage.

Whether I will be willing or not to face a crisis depends on my capacity to see some value issuing from it. If I see that it will provoke greater harm than good, I may hesitate to allow the situation of crisis to touch me. Flight is a likely response as I seek to remove myself from a potentially threatening situation.

If I see crisis, whether psychological or spiritual, as a necessary event in my life, as a time for opening new doors, I will respond differently. The element of fear may remain to a degree. Opening new doors often means closing old ones. In spite of my fear I want to remain open to whatever insights may be brought to light.

This time of crisis can be a time of growth if I am willing to work it through. Crisis implies that I step back and reconsider what I have taken for granted day in and day out. It gives me an opportunity to search for the fundamental meaning of my life and activity. The more honestly and openly I can face myself and others at this time, the more I may gain in spiritual depth.

The life of the spirit is not an evasion of difficulties. It is a gift of the Holy Spirit that allows me to enter into trials and suffering with patience and courage. The Holy Spirit gives me the strength to bypass temporary solutions to crisis and move toward a faith whose vision does not demand solutions but grants me the grace to live in the darkness of not knowing.

The life of personal and spiritual presence to God, since it is a gift, does not depend totally upon an ideal formation period. The Holy Spirit breathes where He will. Nonetheless one cannot deny that the seed of grace which falls on good ground in the novitiate has a better chance of coming to fruition than that which falls on barren ground.

Facing the crisis of religious life and overcoming it from within means that I must first face myself and understand what happens within me when I experience crisis.

Crisis places me in the predicament of being here today and almost anywhere tomorrow. It means instability and insecurity. It can lead to disaster or it can be a challenge that brings me closer to faith and more surrendered to God.

In religious life I often doubt my capacity for spiritual living, for giving myself to God in and through community and apostolate. I experience the anxiety that accompanies doubt. Set before me are my goals and deep within me is the knowledge of my limitations. The deeper I look into myself, the more disintegrated I may feel. Who am I in reality? I may even begin to doubt the reason for my being.

Everyday experience forces me to face new crises. The difficult assignment I feel inadequate to fulfill. My inability to pray. The general feeling of falling apart, physically, mentally, spiritually. The tired bones, confused mind, sagging spirit. This crisis is not heroic or extraordinary. That's what makes the doubt and anxiety more unbearable. Where is this crisis leading me? Do I have the strength to work it through?

When I experience deeply such insecurity, doubt, and anxiety, I may find at long last the God to whom I have committed myself. Without doubt, I cannot experience the need for faith. Without anxiety, I cannot experience God as God and myself as His dependent. Self-sufficiency may blind me to my need to surrender to His grace. Insecurity makes this need starkly real.

I cannot reason myself into this attitude of faith and surrender. I need to experience because of certain circumstances that I cannot go on without faith in God and surrender to His care.

Faith is not lived in the certainty of the future but in the "I don't know" of perseverance. Surrender does not mean that I have everything under control, but rather that "You call the plays, Lord; you support the players."

A crisis for the average person is not one of those rare, heroic "do or die" occasions. It is living in fear and trembling the daily call to faith and surrender.

Recall the plight of the adolescent who realizes that his parents are far from perfect. Because of human inadequacies, they were not able to give him all the love he craved. In the pain of this realization, he can stamp his feet and refuse to grow up until he has received all he has missed. Or he can allow suffering to deepen his ability to give of himself more freely, to love his parents in their imperfect manifestations of love for him.

So too in religious life. Your formation period may not have been perfect for a number of reasons. For example, the novice mistress may not have been prepared properly to assume the delicate task of personal transformation. Nevertheless, if you look with a kindly eye, you can find something of value that you received from her or the other sisters.

Perhaps in prayerful meditation you felt the first faint stirrings of the desire that Christ be the center of your life. Years later, even that positive element can be stamped out if you persist in focusing on what you have missed. Instead of accepting the good you have received, you may reject it because of certain inadequacies. Have you not in this reaction forgotten that the Spirit continues to work within us even under the most averse conditions if we but turn to Him in need and love?

* * *

Formation Centered on the Spiritual

Formation in religious life *as religious* has to be sufficiently centered on the spiritual before religious take up other tasks in the culture like teaching, social work, care for the sick and so on. What if it is not? Is team formation the answer to spiritual formation?

* * *

The similarity between a formation team and an orchestra rests in this: the centering force in each must be the director, the spiritual master in the case of the novitiate, the conductor in the case of the orchestra. Prior to the conductor's appearance each member, oblivious of the other, may play beautiful passages on his instrument, but the effect is chaos. With the appearance of the conductor the concerto takes shape. He unites all the unique sounds into one harmonious whole. A triumph of sound is possible because each member responds to the spirit which moves the conductor.

The spiritual master serves not to create sound but to form religious personalities. The purpose of the spiritual master is to aid the unfolding of religious personalities in the spirit of Christ. As a good conductor knows whether or not the orchestra is capturing the spirit of the music, so too a good director knows whether those being initiated by him are moved by Christ.

Should each candidate work in isolation, oblivious to the centering force of Christ, then initiation into the spiritual life may never get off the ground. The initiates may instead be caught in the struggle for power and popularity. Perhaps a valid test of the value of formation can be likened to a symphony that continues to inspire its listeners throughout the ages.

The religious who has a firm grounding in the spiritual life will grow under the guidance of a wise and balanced master in wisdom and grace before God and man.

In an environment concerned mainly with controlling and manipulating people to its best advantage, I too could become merely a good business manager. The managing me prides itself on being able to respond competently to all occasions. Should my ego operations begin to break down, I am likely to panic. Yet surrender to the Holy may be impossible until I give up my manipulative control of the situation.

In order to come to such an understanding of my true place in God's plan, I must be open to the Spirit. This openness requires discipline, hopefully learned during my formation period. This crucial time must wean me from the world where the managing me has been taught to control life and bring me to the experience of surrender to God.

Humanly speaking, this transformation requires time, guidance, and effort. The number of persons who assist me toward living a life centered on the spiritual is secondary, provided each one is Christ-centered and helps me to reach, with God's grace, that one goal.

I may find that I can speak about my inner life more readily with one person than with another. It is good then to be allowed to do so. If I know how each person is involved in my life from the pre-entrance program on through the years after juniorate, my contact with several persons during my formation period may be beneficial.

However, if true cooperation and a firm spiritual commitment does not exist between all the persons involved in my formation, I may become dispersed rather than centered. Entrusting myself to a number of unqualified persons may impair prayerful growth.

The aim of religious formation is to help the initiate to learn to be present to his own experiences so that he might attain that self-presence and self-acceptance that will dispose him for presence to God. This presence through the formation years hopefully so develops and deepens that it becomes an anchorage for the rest of his religious life.

Silence and solitude aid this coming home to self. Guidance helps the initiate to recognize cultural accretions that could be potential obstacles to religious commitment and fidelity. Which persons and events foster and which hinder his personalization of the attitudes underlying the spirit of the vows?

Formation is thus a highly individualized effort to assist the initiate to come to an experience of his deepest self as present to God. In this process the initiate himself and God have the lead parts. The one who brings them together is the spiritual master.

The master of religious living is not just an educator or a mere dispenser of information but a guide who himself lives this life and who can illumine the way for others. Because his task is so central, thorough preparation is needed for him before he assumes his role. It will be his responsibility to help the novice develop and unfold specifically as a religious.

If the novice master is a real master of religious living, one need not fear an inability to relate to him. The novices, if sincere, can put aside personality preferences. They are able to accept him as one who knows the way better than they and who himself seems to be travelling it. All the novices can thus relate to him, for through and with him, they can begin to find their own way.

Individual children and adolescents reach physical maturity at a time which is different for each person. Factors entering into this maturation process include sex, environmental and physical conditions, and bodily structure; each plays its part. Even in the same family all the boys and all the girls do not mature physically or emotionally at the same pace.

By analogy, the religious who enter a community do not come to lived spirituality in the same way and in the same amount of time. Home life, spiritual direction, individual personality differences are some factors that enter into the process of spiritual maturation. It is unnatural to set up a rigid model for spiritual growth and expect all to follow it.

Possibly some religious can grow in spirit in spite of a rigid model, but there is the equal possibility that others could be completely stifled and hindered by adherence to such a model.

Many formation programs have stipulated periods of time wherein the maturing process is expected to take place before the religious takes on tasks in the culture like teaching, social work, care for the sick, and so on.

The ideal to strive for is to concentrate specifically on individuals, not to apply general norms to all religious in a given community.

To provide some mature religious as resource people in the formation program is desirable, provided they offer no major obstacle to the spiritual master, who is the general coordinator of the formation program. The history of vowed religious living in both East and West bears testimony to the absolute necessity of his presence and authority.

The old proverb, "Too many cooks spoil the soup," bears much truth in the mysterious process of spiritual formation.

It is not possible to give "the answer" to the living process we call spiritual formation. Nonetheless, the need we feel for such an answer is indicative of our plight. In our panic we search for an answer: the present solution seems to be a formation team.

Our mistake lies not in the effort to find religious who can cooperate with one another in the task of formation, but rather in the belief that any one plan or project in and by itself can change our lives.

There are no definite answers for living. When we speak of problems and solutions, we are speaking out of the realm of the intellect. Here we can consciously analyze ideas, develop critical thinking, reasonably combine a multiplicity of proposals into an acceptable and comprehensive whole. All of this is an essential part of living, but human life encompasses much more than the planning intellect alone.

Growth of the human spirit is not under the power of our conscious control; it takes place underground, so to speak. When the seed planted in the earth ruptures, its new life can begin. Paradoxically, we begin to live when we experience a kind of death to the old self. Reborn in Christ, we begin to mature as quietly and imperceptibly as a young plant.

At moments we experience the wholeness of our lives, but this wholeness is not subject to logical analysis. Joy and sorrow, trust and fear, love and hostility open us to the mystery of our spiritual life, its beauty and paradox.

When Christ lives in our hearts through faith, our hidden selves grow strong in his Spirit. We have the strength to grasp the breadth and the length, the height and the depth because He is our strength, until knowing the love of Christ which is beyond all knowledge, we are filled with the utter fullness of god. (Ephesians 3:14-19)

* * *

Encountering the Essential in Religious Life

How can we better prepare novices now entering religious life to encounter fellow religious whose training in the past was different with regard to what is essential to religious life?

* * *

The worst way to prepare novices for their future encounter with fellow religious who differ from them in their concept of what is essential to religious life would be to concentrate on preparing them for this encounter. Such a preparation might create problems of a "generation gap" that is not really there.

An approach like this frequently produces a group of crusaders who, oblivious of tact or timing, descend on already insecure and suspicious senior sisters causing increased conflict and suspicion.

Another approach is to dissolve the traditional

separation between novices and the senior professed in the hope that prolonged proximity will generate understanding. We may then find a novice with as yet little or no experience of what is fundamental and what is peripheral in religious life, trying to make sense of the conflicting views rampant in her community and eventually falling in line with one or the other faction.

Preparation for the future is best achieved by authentic living in the present. The best preparation for a joyful childhood is the experience of having been cared for as an infant; the fitting prologue to adulthood is a realistic adolescence. One is therefore inclined to reason that the best preparation for encountering older religious in community life is the experience of having encountered oneself and fellow novices in the novitiate.

Compassion for the blindness of others is impossible if one has never known what it is to grope in darkness. Paradoxically, the novice who is best prepared to encounter the differences in others is the one who knows that she is never really prepared and that compassion and understanding must be creatively wrought anew in each new situation.

If the vision of religious life which I as a novice have received is truly a vision and not a mirage, I know that I am called to live humbly and compassionately with others who may not see as I see. If I find that I have no patience with or understanding of another's seemingly stubborn attachment to non-essentials, I may suspect that what I cling to is not a vision of the fundamental, but another set of non-essentials—the 1977 instead of the 1877 variety!

Contemporary religious life is undergoing profound, even revolutionary changes. With the increasing polarization of religious communities into old school and new school groups, how one is to unite young and old is a question of vital importance.

If the formation of the young springs from the roots of religious living, the problem of future division is bound to diminish. A formation that springs from these roots transcends the narrow, divisive categories of conservative and liberal. Its emphasis on living in presence to the Holy and radiating this presence in one's work, play, and prayer builds a bridge whereby young and old can meet in spiritual communion.

Genuine religious formation creates a deep respect for each person, with all his goodness, fears, doubts, and hesitations. If this attitude is lived and not just an abstract theory, a young religious will not be surprised when he discovers that some older and even some younger religious look at religious life in a way that differs from his own view.

In the process of formation under a well formed director, the initiate learns not to turn aside from these people but to recognize, beyond their fear, persons who are asking to be met and loved. A persevering love gradually reduces fears so that both sides can see how close to one another they really are.

Some kind of program for the older members of the community may be initiated in which they are brought up to date on the renewed spirituality of religious living. This program also affords an acquaintance with the formation currently being given to the younger members. Both groups may thus find their fears and suspicions dissolving.

Far from wrecking religious life, the profound changes it is undergoing will make it an even more effective force for preserving lived spirituality in today's world.

"Putting up" with others implies a kind of condescension, if not haughtiness. Living in community necessitates a reverent and respectful attitude, not a condescending one. If my training is different from that of another religious, this is all the more reason to listen respectfully to her. No age has a monopoly on insight. The more we differ, the more we must listen.

There are many perspectives and each holds considerable truth. If we merely put up with the other's view, may not the same haughty attitude characterize our presence to God?

Encounters with others are much more full than what we realize. Abstract thinking and conceptualizations are important but, beyond the verbal encounter, there is a whole space of living that speaks as strongly, if not more strongly, than our words. Words are only a small part of the total reality of human encounter.

The way I help another, the way she helps me, may say more than our accompanying words, if any.

By developing a sense of openness whether I am novice or professed, I may find that element of concern which brings us closer than any abstract generalizations or learned encounter techniques.

In the past, preparation for full incorporation into a religious congregation tended to be more practice than person-centered.

The more structured approach of the past often resulted in an emphasis on external conformity to the detriment of interior growth. Now the influx of relevant knowledge gleaned from the human and social sciences has led to a more intense awareness of the uniqueness of each person's call from God. As a result, some of the more rigid group norms are being deemphasized. This in no way diminishes the good effect they may have had in previous years; it merely indicates that they are not the most effective means of deepening interiority today.

More important than the what received in formation is the who receiving.

Novices, enriched by the spiritual and intellectual formation available to them, ought to appreciate even more the good will and personal sacrifice of their senior sisters.

Senior sisters must accept without jealousy or envy the numerous opportunities for personal and spiritual growth denied them which the new members of the community may enjoy.

Each sister, able to respect her own uniqueness, with her limitations and talents before God, will also be able to respect others for the individuality they possess. Preparation for encounter is then based on persons rather than on practices.

Lived experience reveals that the phenomena of "living out of one's head" or living in a verbal universe is not foreign to the contemporary religious. The crux of the matter is that members of a religious community do not always share the same verbal universes. The world of a younger sister may be one of caring and sharing, dialogue, freedom, personal responsibility and involvement while the world of her superior may be one of self-abnegation, community loyalty, and striving for perfection.

It is evident that the verbal universes of both religious are laudable. Likewise it is clear that conflict is bound to occur between these two well meaning persons. Each has her separate vision of how things ought to be. The experience of religious living is a dynamic flow of interactions that draws upon such fundamental religious attitudes as patience, understanding, respect and the humility to tolerate the conflicts and imperfections of every human situation.

Reality, the way things are and not the way they should be, presents us with concrete conflicts. Novices have to cope with lived reality. They cannot take refuge in verbal universes in the name of freedom and responsibility.

For example, a novice may absent herself from recreation because she is not feeling disposed to be sociable, or she may follow the guidance of the Spirit and go to chapel only when drawn to pray. While these attitudes may be occasionally permitted, the novice who is constantly affirmed in this stand, soon lives in a conflictless distortion of reality.

In order to prepare her for encounter with older religious, it is necessary to insist that she live in touch with obligations as a novice and respond patiently and obediently to conflicts that will inevitably ensue. In this she may be exposed to the test of reality. If she passes, then novitiate may become a time of maturing personally and spiritually and not just a prolongation of her earlier adolescent or childhood life.

* * *

Necessity of Structure in the Novitiate

Do you see the necessity of greater structure during the novitiate so that a religious has the strength to sustain his life as religious in the post-novitiate years? The current feeling is that it is too difficult to impose structure on today's youth. How is the dilemma of structure solved without going to one or the other extreme: too many structures, no structures?

* * *

Why did you as a young person embrace Christian religious life rather than Christian marriage?

At one precious time in your life, you felt called. You were moved by the mystery of a love greater than yourself. Into the silent void of your heart, God spoke His word. You could do nothing but follow, if you were to be true to yourself and to Him. Then your response to this call took flesh and found expression in the act of embracing a structure.

This structure provided a concrete way of life, organized and institutionalized, to express and nourish the deep mystery of the call experienced in your heart.

In the light of your past experience, you can understand the profound and reciprocal implications of desire and structure, of charism and institution.

Originally you chose a specific structure because you sensed that it would help you make concrete an inner experience, a felt need to give your life to God. Through wholehearted living of the structures of religious life, you attempted to embody the inner experience of your call to love and serve the Lord. From the structures of this life, you expected to receive the freedom you needed to share your experience of this call with others.

When faced, then, with today's constant questioning of the structures of religious life, the young initiate as well as the professed religious might do well to remember the original experience and grace of her vocation. Such prayerful remembrance can illumine once again the purpose of structure in our lives, for structure exists to express and foster our original and ongoing experience of the Spirit.

The dilemma of structure is not a question of "how much" or "how little," but a means by which we can with ease and confidence turn to the God who first called and encountered us in Christ. When this encounter with the living God is both personal and communal, both alive and growing in depth, we will be able to accept, reject, or change structures in accordance with the wisdom that comes from our worshipful stance to God. Then structures will not entangle us in complicated webs but tune in to the inner music of our souls.

Good structures, like good soul music, well up from the depths of a man while they articulate and deepen the inner mystery of his life. Such structures, far from binding us, free us for the great adventure of lived communion with God, which is at the core of religious living.

The expression, "to impose structure", reminds us of a

cookie-cutter making an imprint on the dough. To impose a structure without sufficient preparation may encourage exterior conformity without fostering inner commitment to Christ.

Rather than give the novice strength to sustain her religious life in post-novitiate years, she may be inclined to shed impersonalized structures like a butterfly sheds its cocoon. She may see such structures merely as a passing phase of her religious life rather than the necessary supports they are.

Does this mean that congregations should abandon structures on the ground that young people are not accustomed to them?

This discarding may be a denial of the very reasons young people enter religious life. A young person seeking admission to religious life today expects to be initiated into a life different from her former life style. She anticipates a life that will foster her presence to God and enable her to be a source of religious inspiration for those who participate with her in various fields of cultural endeavor.

Her formation can be viewed from the outside, as a "uniform" she puts on, or from the inside as a bringing forth of self, as a giving of form to her inner being. Structures should serve the second way. Then they become guidelines along which the novice gives form to her personal commitment to Christ.

The initiate to religious life needs the support of meaningful structure if he is to sink his roots into this new life style. The main purpose of external structure ought to be the formation of internal structure.

To be ruled by a mere mechanical and routine adherence to structure is always wrong. The candidate must see the true purpose of structure or at least trust this purpose until it becomes evident to her.

Avoiding direction may be as destructive to the initiate as

it is to the community as a whole. On the other hand, imposing structure for its own sake, without helping the initiate to see its value for his life, is no solution. The young religious must be led to see experientially the value of those structures which provide time for prayer, solitude, and creative leisure. He comes from a culture in which noise and activity often crowd out the deeper experiences of life.

The formation directors must help him to understand why his new life cannot be filled with the constant blare of the radio, the incessant chatter of others, the high degree of activity of his former life.

In solitude he may come to a better understanding of himself, others, and God and thus discover the true meaning of his life.

Structures whose only purpose seems to be to regiment the community or to maintain an acceptable public image may rightly be rejected by the candidate. The community must look realistically at its structures to see if they contribute to the development of the religious person as a whole, to his personal as well as spiritual needs.

Gradually the young candidate will build out of external structures sound internal structures to safeguard his spiritual life. External structures become less essential to him. However, he is neither opposed to nor threatened by external structure. If structures are lenient, his life will still be lived in harmony with his religious commitment.

When a child begins to write, his teacher does not simply give him pencil and paper and then sit back expecting him to produce an original manuscript. The child must learn slowly and with deliberate effort the elementary mechanics of tracing out individual letters, of joining these letters to make words and those words to make thoughts.

The child sees little purpose in sitting hour after hour at his desk with feet flat on the floor, paper slanted at a definite angle, copying and recopying onto his own sheet the example of the letters before him. He may be eager to learn to write, but he never expected writing to be so mundane, so demanding, so painstakingly slow a process. And yet the teacher knows that there is no other way to be a fluent and gifted writer than to begin in this mundane way.

The novice, too, needs to learn slowly, in step-by-step fashion, the ways of the Lord working within her. Her aspirations to be a good religious may cloud her perception of what really is going on within her. So she needs to be led in this unfolding of her spiritual self by a wise novice directress. She has much to discover about herself, about the Lord, and about the wonderful and mysterious relationship she so boldly hopes to form with Him. She needs to learn that her life is His doing much more than it is her own.

External helps that facilitate this learning process in the young religious are referred to as structures. Because the need for such help is great at the outset of religious life, the need for structures is that much greater.

As the young child grows up and gains more and more ease in writing, he no longer has to be held to set patterns. He gradually writes more freely, with grace and style. So, too, as the novice grows, the religious orientation of life takes a firmer grip upon her. She begins to interiorize the rhythm and discipline which the structures of the novitiate endeavor to insure for her. She may, under continual spiritual direction, move on to new means to assure her growth as a religious.

Throughout this period, and indeed throughout her life, structures are seen not as obstacles to religious living but as the stepping-stones given her to reach the One she wishes to serve.

Structure is never in itself any guarantee that one will live religiously in post-novitiate days. It is God's grace and my cooperation with this grace which gives me strength to persevere in my chosen way of life.

The time of novitiate, like the time of any new experience in life, demands form and discipline to free the person for those higher goals he came here to pursue. More important than the type of structure is how the young religious is initiated into the meaning of structure for her religious life. The novitiate is the time when religious must learn the lesson of seeing beyond the imposition of structure to its deeper meaning for life.

Youth today are caught in our culture's split over the issue of structure and authority and profit by such questioning, for in grappling with the issue of structure the novice herself may come to the conclusion that there can be no real growth without it.

AFTERWORD

By Adrian van Kaam

Having come to the end of this book, you have hopefully begun to reflect upon your life direction in light of questions and answers about such basics of Christian living as acceptance of self, commitment to Christ, prayer and surrender. You may now be feeling the need to come to a more personal answer to these questions—one that would be in tune with your own unique life direction. This latter theme has become central in our work at the Institute. We take it up in courses and seminars and have especially focused on it in THE DYNAMICS OF SPIRITUAL SELF DIRECTION (Denville, N.J.: Dimension Books, 1976). We would like, therefore, to conclude this book by relating its contents to some additional reflections on the art and discipline of spiritual self direction.

As you may have gathered from the answers in this book, your life as a Christian lay person—married or single—as a priest or religious has a unique destiny in the Lord Jesus. Becoming conscious of this calling through spiritual reading and meditation will help you to unfold continually as a valuable member of the Body of Christ, as an effective citizen of his Kingdom. No longer will you be tempted to undergo life passively, like an actor in a Greek tragedy. Instead you will feel inspired to mold your destiny creatively. The more you grow in the life of commitment, prayer, and surrender, the more you will realize that the grace of Christ deepens immensely your potential for responsible self unfolding. Commitment to Christ and the will of the Father releases in you the power of self emergence. This potential for self direction lies at the heart of your humanness. Without it you can never know who you are and never come to creative self unfolding in Christ.

Self direction in light of the Spirit has lately become a

much more personal endeavor. In the past you were sustained in this search by a universal Christian culture. Since the secularization of modern life, however, you are exposed to countless views and forms of life you would not have known about in the uniform Christian culture of the past. You now have to find your way as a modern Christian in the world by permeating and transfiguring cultural styles and forms that are not directly of Christian origin. Like many others, you may feel overwhelmed with the options presented to you today. At times you may feel paralyzed; at others you may run bewildered in many directions. You ask yourself how can I find my way as a creative Christian in the new wide open situation of a diaspora Christianity? How can I live the essential message of the faith in my own style, now that there is no longer a uniform code to tell me in detail how to incarnate Christ in my life and world? How can I develop the inner security and emotional maturity that make it possible to find my way in this bewildering society?

In a world of increasing options and escalating change, it is understandable that you find yourself confused about how to grow towards your unique destiny in the Lord. The secular world in which you live is dynamic, fascinating, seductive. At times you may be beguiled by its grandiose projects. You begin then to grow according to its arbitrary enthusiasms rather than growing as a self directed Christian in accordance with your graced inspirations.

Admittedly the present day wide open secular society is a confusion of paradigms and life styles. Yet you can also look at it in a positive way. Society today offers a greater variety of possibilities to incarnate the life of Christ in the modern world; it enables Christian spirituality to reveal itself in a richness of forms undreamt of before. In a sense all these choices make it easier for you to find your own peculiar niche in the Father's house where the many rooms promised by Jesus are now becoming manifest.

To find your way requires, however, that you seek a transcendent platform from which to contemplate in quiet the many options offered to you. Your platform is the word of Christ in the Church, Holy Scripture, and spiritual masters. Reflect on these words, as you have reflected on the questions and answers in this book. Assimilate them as Mary did when she pondered the words of Jesus in her heart. Such prayerful reflection becomes like a lighthouse that illumines the choppy sea of secular projects, a beam that outlines the treacherous cliffs on which the ship of your life might otherwise be dashed to pieces.

In His light you become aware that you often forge ahead in directions that have no real meaning for your life because they are at odds with your inner divine self direction. Outside that direction you lose the concrete sense of who you are and, the more lost you become, the more desperately you begin to search for substitutes. You may rush after every fad that comes along. Enchanted by the newest and the latest, you try to keep up with a world that without the Holy Spirit does not know where it is going. You may become so adept at reacting that you forget how to respond out of an inner at oneness with the Lord and His word and with your unique calling within that word. You try to adopt new life styles, to be in with what is current; you begin to define yourself mainly in terms of your occupations and hobbies. Instead of knowing who you are, you ask yourself how your neighbors value you. You become your secular roles to gain the approval of the world and you betray the Christian in yourself who has to penetrate and transfigure these roles. You take on new and alien patterns of living, yet you do not try to harmonize them with your spiritual values. You slide along or are swept along, bewitched by the media, beguiled by the sophistication of your secular peers. You let others tell you who you are and you end up in cheap conformity to the impressive ways of those who do well in this world.

The Spirit inside you may have used this book to make you sense that something is wrong. While reading these pages, He may have made you feel that you are on a merry-go-round of assumed directions not really your own. You begin perhaps to realize that superficial adaptations to what is "in" today and "gone" tomorrow make it impossible for you to find out who you are. You may realize that you often felt empty, frustrated, lost, and lonely. The questions and answers of fellow Christians—lay and religious—read in this book may have led you to a moment of stillness. You may have heard the Spirit cry out to you. You may suddenly realize that you are out of touch with your deepest self. You may even have experienced panic or apathy.

You may now come to the insight that the secular society offers no permanent guidelines for inner growth. Only Christ and the masters of the spiritual life who lived in His light can tell you who you are. To be faithful to your life direction is not a static knowing but a dynamic quest. You emerge by changing yourself in dialogue with the modern world, but this dialogue takes place in light of the Holy Spirit. In His light you select and integrate such changes in what you already know to be God's will for you. Real self emergence is, after all, a transition from the old to the new in a way that makes sense to your inner self in Christ. But nothing will make sense until you know as much as you can about yourself as called forth by God. You must explore His work in yourself, reaffirm His direction of your life. Only then may you sense where to go and how to get there in a way that is right for the unique person you are.

Self emergence in Christ always implies change, but it should be a change you choose to make, in a direction you choose to go because you see where the Father's will is calling you. Instead of being carried along powerless and without control by the pace of this world, you can elect, with the grace of God, to take hold of your life. Instead of following someone else's prescriptions for success in this world or getting lost in the shuffle, you can learn how to make new possibilities of incarnation serve the coming of the Kingdom in yourself and others. If you choose not to go along with certain fads and fashions, you at least know it is your own choice in deference to God's holy will. You must participate in secular life selectively and uniquely, keeping in touch with your divine life direction and with your ongoing emergence in Christ. This is the only way in which adaptation to the world can benefit society without loss of your unique direction in the Lord or diminishment of your presence to the Eternal Love that carries us.